THE
DIVORCE
ORGANIZER
& PLANNER

BRETTE McWHORTER SEMBER

McGraw·Hill

New York   Chicago   San Francisco   Lisbon   London   Madrid   Mexico City
Milan   New Delhi   San Juan   Seoul   Singapore   Sydney   Toronto

Library of Congress Cataloging-in-Publication Data

Sember, Brette McWhorter, 1968–
    The divorce organizer and planner / Brette McWhorter Sember.
        p.   cm.
    ISBN 0-07-142961-1 (alk. paper)
    1. Divorce suits—United States—Popular works.   I. Title.

  KF535.Z9S46   2004
  346.7301′66—dc22   2003022341

3 4 5 6 7 8 9 0 AGM/AGM 3 2 1 0 9 8 7

ISBN 0-07-142961-1

Interior design by Nick Panos

McGraw-Hill books are available at special quantity discounts to use as premiums and sales promotions, or for use in corporate training programs. For more information, please write to the Director of Special Sales, Professional Publishing, McGraw-Hill, Two Penn Plaza, New York, NY 10121-2298. Or contact your local bookstore.

"This publication is designed to provide accurate and authoritative information in regard to the subject matter covered. It is sold with the understanding that the publisher and author are not engaged in rendering legal, accounting, or other professional service. If legal advice or other expert assistance is required, the services of a competent professional person should be sought."

—From the Declaration of Principles jointly adopted by a Committee
of the American Bar Association and a Committee of Publishers and Associations

This book is printed on acid-free paper.

Contents

v

Contents

Acknowledgments

It's hard to write the acknowledgments page because it means that this project has come to an end. My heartfelt thanks go to Michele Pezzuti, my wonderful editor, who has a certain genius with manuscripts, and to Sheree Bykofsky, my faithful agent, who got this book to where it is. Many thanks also to Megan Buckley and Janet Rosen, who saw the potential in the book, were always positive about it, and helped it find a home. My dear friend Belle Wong, who was there every day with support and a shoulder to complain on, got me through the rough patches. As always, my love and thanks go to my husband, Terry, who has always been my biggest fan, and to Quinne and Zayne, who are the true lights in my world.

Introduction

Nothing about divorce is easy. You're going through emotional ups and downs, rearranging your living accommodations, dealing with financial problems, helping your kids cope, and trying to get through the confusing legal maze that is ahead of you. The last thing you probably want to do is focus on the nitty-gritty paperwork, but getting organized is one of the best ways to get through your divorce. Despite the many difficult emotions it involves, a divorce is really a business transaction. Business transactions that are handled in an organized and careful way tend to be successful. Because you are struggling with so many emotions during a divorce, it is often hard to think clearly, but you need a clear mind to ensure that you cover all the details. Getting what you want is often a function of presenting enough solid evidence to support your request, whether it is custody, child support, alimony, or a property settlement. This book will help you do that.

Divorces are all about paperwork. Everything except oral testimony must be presented to the court in writing. You will have to gather a lot of information about assets, debts, and property for your attorney, and you will have to organize it carefully. If you hand over an envelope stuffed with papers that have been thrown together, your attorney will have to spend time sorting through them, and you will be billed for that time. The more organized you are, the more you can reduce your attorney costs.

You also need to document issues such as visitation problems, household items that need to be divided, phone calls, names of people who can testify on your behalf, and the like. When you put the information on paper, you can arrange it in an easy-to-follow format and present it to your attorney. If you don't write things down, you have to explain them from memory when you meet with your attorney or talk on the phone. You may not be sure if your attorney understands what you're saying, and you could forget to mention some key points. This book helps you avoid miscommunication.

This may be one of the most confusing times in your life. Many people in your situation don't know what to do to improve their chances at custody or a better settlement. They are overwhelmed by the sheer amount of paperwork involved. Using the forms and organizational tools in this book, you will learn not only how to organize important documents and records, but also how to create logs that will help your attorney prove your case and get the outcome you desire. It is one thing to know that your spouse has violated a temporary order of visitation. It is quite another to be able to hand your attorney a detailed log containing the dates, times, and details of each violation. The more detailed your records are, the easier it is for your attorney to present your case to the court.

When you have worked your way through this book, you will have created a detailed record that your attorney can use to complete court documents and to present your case effectively. Feel free to make copies of the forms and lists provided in this book. You may want to use some of them over and over again as you work through the divorce process. You may need to modify certain forms as your divorce progresses.

The book includes tips on how to select and work with an attorney, how to prepare yourself for court, what to do once your divorce is finalized, and much more. You will be well prepared for all of the meetings and court proceedings ahead of you. And you will find that being organized and prepared will make a huge difference in the way you feel, the expenses you incur, and the outcome you get.

Getting and Staying Organized

Getting organized is the single most important thing you can do to ensure that your attorney will be able to represent you well, that the court will see your side of the story, and that you will be able to cope with the divorce and all the work it entails. Staying organized isn't always easy, but it is always helpful.

Dealing with Emotions

Your emotions are a major hurdle to remaining organized and developing a strategy for your divorce. Divorce is one of the most traumatic events of your life. You are going to feel confused, hurt, angry, frustrated, frightened, over-loaded, and sad. It is hard to control your overpowering emotions when meeting with your lawyer, listening to half-truths and misrepresentations in court, communicating with your spouse and the opposing attorney, and facing all of the divorce-related paperwork. But these emotions will only get in the way of what is essentially a complicated business transaction—your divorce.

The best thing you can do is to deal with your emotions so they do not interfere with the difficult work ahead. This doesn't mean you have to suppress your feelings. It does mean you should approach your divorce with a cool and calculated mind-set that will allow you to keep clear records, deal with your attorney, negotiate with your spouse, and get through court appearances. You can't do that if your emotions are out of control. You're likely to miss things when you make emotional decisions.

Do whatever you need to do to get through the emotional part of the divorce—see a counselor, talk to friends, spend time with your family, and so on—but don't allow your emotions to interfere with the careful planning and organizing you must do. Try to keep the business part of the divorce separate from the emotional part. The Appendix lists resources that can help you cope with these tangled feelings.

Deciding What You Want

Many people come into the divorce process still uncertain if a divorce is the answer for them. If you have any doubts, talk to your spouse and see a counselor or marriage therapist. You cannot proceed efficiently through the divorce process if you are unsure whether divorce is the best avenue.

Decision making is an integral part of the divorce process. You need to determine what you want in terms of custody, alimony, child support, property division, and debt. This book will help you identify and organize all of the information that affects these key decisions. It won't help you determine what your goals are in the divorce. That is something you will need to think long and hard about.

Some of the decisions ahead will be very difficult to make, while others will seem obvious. You will change your mind about some decisions several times. You might not always find the perfect solution, simply because the perfect solution doesn't exist. Try to stay focused and take decisions one at a time. Realize that while these decisions are important, they are not the end of the world. Try to keep your perspective. No matter what happens, you will survive the divorce process and get on with your life.

Developing an Organizational System

This book is designed to help you organize the information that affects your divorce. You will find that in order to work with the system set up in this book, you have to make a commitment to being organized in all areas of your life.

Being organized will reduce your stress level and give you a feeling of control over the divorce process. It can save you time and money as you work through the process.

Being organized does not mean being anal or compulsive. It does, however, mean that you will have to devote some time to organizing and creating records. Once you understand what you need to obtain, it is easy to maintain the system.

To get organized, you need to develop routines that ensure you will keep information in the proper places. Make it a habit, for example, to record the date, time, and content of phone calls with your spouse. Make it second nature to reach for the phone log as soon as you hang up. Put bills in the same place after paying them. Record child support payments when you write or deposit the check. Creating routines will help you keep records without having to think about it.

Saving Money Through Organization

Training yourself to remain organized throughout the divorce process will help you save money. Your attorney is paid by the hour (and probably is billing you at the rate of $150 an hour or more). He or she bills you in five-, ten-, or fifteen-minute increments and always rounds up! Anything you do to reduce the amount of time your attorney has to spend on your case will reduce your costs.

Attorneys spend a lot of time explaining to their divorce clients what documents they need to provide; how to keep records for visitation and child support; and how to create lists of assets, budgets, and so on. This book gives you a huge head start by helping you collect, organize, and record all of this information into a format that you can easily photocopy and give to your attorney. This will save your attorney's time and your money.

Keeping a Calendar

You probably already keep a calendar for household or business appointments. You might have a wall calendar on which you and your family record school and sports events. You might also use an appointment book or PDA in your job. But because your divorce is going to infiltrate every aspect of your life, you need to keep a master calendar on which you record everything. Weekly or monthly calendars work well for this purpose and can be found at office supply or discount stores.

The master calendar will list your children's appointments; your personal and business appointments; and all your divorce-related meetings, court appearances, and deadlines. Having a master calendar is important because your meetings with attorneys and court appearances might sometimes conflict with your family or business obligations. You need to have everything in front of you when dates are being scheduled so that you can immediately speak up and let everyone know when you are unavailable.

It's also important to keep a complete calendar to use as evidence should you ever need to prove where you or your children were at certain times. Keeping track of school events you attend, as well as times the children are with you or your spouse, will give you a simple history of how you and your children spent your time. See Chapter 14 for more information about this.

Tips for Managing a Master Calendar

You may not want to cart your new master calendar around with you to work, to swim meets, or to the doctor's office. Continue to use your other calendars, but at the end of every day make it a point to transfer newly scheduled events to the master calendar.

When you record divorce-related matters on the calendar, make sure you clearly record the place and time of the appointment or appearance. Indicate what room number it will be held in and whether the time is A.M. or P.M.

You can also use the calendar to record deadlines. Your attorney will give you papers to complete at several points along the way. Find out when he or she needs them completed by and put that date on your calendar. Make sure you write a clear explanation on the calendar! A scribbled note that says "papers" might make sense to you now, but it won't be as clear in two weeks or a month.

Calendar Review

Check your calendar at the beginning of each week (either on Sunday or on Monday morning). Review what is scheduled or due in the coming week. This

4

way you won't suddenly realize on Thursday night that you have to get a financial affidavit back to your attorney on Friday when you haven't even begun to work on it. Make it a point to check your calendar every morning so you know where you need to be that day and when. You might be certain that your meeting is at four o'clock when it was really scheduled for two o'clock. It's easy to mix up times and dates in the course of your normal busy life, but it's even easier to do when you're under emotional stress.

Some people have a tendency to forget appointments or confuse times for things they dread or are uncomfortable about. If this is the case for you, you'll have to work extra hard to stay on top of things. Judges are rather unforgiving when it comes to scheduling mistakes.

Using To-Do Lists

Some people are natural list makers, while others never use lists. Whichever category you fall into, you'll find that list making is an efficient way to help you get things done and stay organized during your divorce. You're going to have a lot of details to deal with, and the best way to keep track of them is to put them in writing. Lists ease the strain of trying to remember every detail. Your list can be your memory.

Types of To-Do Lists

There are lots of ways to structure to-do lists. You'll need to choose the types that work best for you.

Daily or Weekly Lists

Some people find that making a list of everything that has to get done on a certain day or during a week helps them to stay focused and on target. Having a long list of things to get done over the course of a month or a few weeks doesn't help you find a way to move through the list. Breaking down the tasks and assigning a time in which each will be completed helps you get things done in an orderly way and manage your time so you can fit everything into your schedule. A sample daily list might include:

- bring home pay stubs from desk
- call Mom about babysitting
- call lawyer about changing the locks
- go to bank

You might find it helpful to make a master list of everything you need to do in a certain week and then assign the items on that list to specific days of the week. That way if you don't get through your daily list, the item still appears on the weekly list and won't be forgotten.

Topic-Oriented Lists

Sometimes it is helpful to make lists organized by topics. For example, you might make one list that focuses on household duties. It might include:

- get out box of memorabilia to divide
- pick up empty boxes
- call real-estate agent
- mow lawn

Another list might be for divorce paperwork:

- call credit card company for missing statement
- find 401(k) papers
- locate marriage license
- make copies of kids' social security cards

6   *Managing To-Do Lists*

It's easy to make to-do lists and then forget about them, but these lists will work only if you use them. Keep your list where you can see it, and cross things off when you complete them. Check the list regularly so you don't forget any items. If you use a PDA or computer, make sure you check the lists there as well.

To increase the effectiveness of your lists, you may wish to keep them with your master calendar. You can coordinate your weekly activities and manage your to-do list at the same time. A blank to-do list is included at the end of this chapter.

Managing Documents

You're going to be up to your ears in paperwork as you go through your divorce. Not only will there be correspondence and paperwork from your attorney, but there will also be lots of paperwork you'll be solely responsible for, such as name changes on accounts, notifications to schools, and everything else that is involved in separating one set of finances into two.

It can be overwhelming to deal with all the forms and papers that will come your way during the divorce process, but if you develop a system that lets you take control of them, you'll feel calmer. You'll also feel confident that everything is in a place where you can easily find it.

Accordion Folders

You need to keep track of court papers, of course, but you should also keep track of papers related to household expenses, income, debts, items you own, and more. To get started, purchase an accordion-style folder that you will use in conjunction with this book. Try to buy a plastic accordion folder. Since you will be carrying it with you to meetings and appointments, you want it to be sturdy. You may need to purchase two folders if you can't find one with enough pockets. You will need at least sixteen pockets. You can also use a plastic box with file folders. (File boxes and accordian folders can be found at office supply stores.) Take the file with you to every meeting with your attorney and every court appearance. As you use this book, you will file papers in the folder and have them readily available so that you can find what you need quickly.

Label the dividers in your folder with the following headings:

Household Inventory
Documents to Complete for Attorney
Documents from Attorney/Court Papers
Attorney Bills and Receipts
Documents from Other Professionals
Household Documents
Income Documents

Monthly Expenses
Large Assets
Debts
Children's Expenses
Children's Uninsured Health Care Receipts
Child Support Receipts
Alimony Receipts
Evidence from Witnesses
Property Distribution Receipts

As you work through this book, you will learn how to use each pocket.

Household Paperwork

You probably already have some kind of system in place for managing household paperwork, but because so many of these documents are going to be important in your divorce, take a minute to think about your organizational system.

If you haven't already done so, identify one specific place where you will put all your important papers. You know how it is when you open the mail or your children hand you papers from school. You set the information aside until you have time to deal with it, but things are easily lost or forgotten this way. Pick one place where you will put incoming mail. A wire basket works well, or a spot on a desk, counter, or bookcase.

Go through the stack once a week to pay bills and fill out forms that are due. Then file everything else where you can find it again easily. A two-drawer file cabinet is ideal for this. Label a folder for every company or organization you deal with such as the electric company, school, cable company, health insurance carrier, bank, and so on.

If you don't have a file cabinet, use a plastic box with file folders in it or an expandable file folder with compartments that can be labeled. It doesn't matter where you put the papers, as long as you put them somewhere. It's important to distinguish between old accounts and new accounts. For example, if the electric bill was in both names and is now in one name only, start a separate file for the single account. Do the same thing for credit cards, bank accounts, and so on. Create labels that are specific to what is in the file. For example, electric bills should be filed under the name of the company, not under *L* for "lights." Using appropriate labels will make your documents easier to find.

Other General Organizational Tips

Here are a few more organizational and management tips to help you get through the divorce:

- **Always leave early for appointments.** You might have trouble finding the courthouse or finding parking. You don't want to be late.
- **Continue to eat and drink on a normal schedule.** You will feel out of sorts and confused if you skip meals.
- **Retain normalcy in your life.** Go to the gym, have dinner with the kids, go out with friends, and take care of household chores. Keeping a normal routine will help you stay focused and feel like you are living a normal life.
- **Try to maintain a nonconfrontational attitude with your spouse.** Divorce is all about conflict, but if you can minimize the conflicts you go through, you will feel less stressed out and better able to cope with the ones that can't be avoided.
- **Take the issues involved in your divorce one at a time and focus on solutions rather than problems.** If you look at the divorce as a whole, it can seem overwhelming, but if you deal with one step at a time it will be more manageable.
- **Stop looking behind you.** You can't change the past, but you can deal with the present and plan for the future. Focus on what you can affect.
- **Give yourself a break.** You're not perfect, and you're even less likely to be perfect when you're going through a divorce. If you expect too much of yourself, you're going to feel let down if you can't meet those high expectations.
- **Don't make things into a crisis.** Take a step back and try to get some perspective. Remember, this is just one small section of your life, and it will soon be over.

9 ▶

- **Develop routines that will help you get things done.** Always do the laundry on Monday nights, set out lunch money the night before, put your keys in one place, and so on. Even if you were not a routine-oriented person before the divorce, try to be now.
- **Be in charge of your divorce; don't let your divorce be in charge of you.** This book helps you grab hold of the reins and direct the process. Don't let yourself fall into passivity. Make decisions, take actions, and ask questions.

TO-DO LIST

Make copies of this list for further use.

To-Do List for _____ (date or week)

_____

_____

_____

_____

_____

_____

_____

_____

_____

_____

_____

_____

_____

_____

_____

_____

_____

_____

_____

_____

_____

_____

_____

_____

2

Protecting Yourself

No matter how amicable your divorce is, or seems, you must prepare yourself for the worst. Many people start a divorce thinking it will be fast and friendly, only to find out that their spouse is using underhanded tactics, isn't being completely honest, or is breaking agreements.

Protecting yourself in your divorce means planning for the worst while hoping for the best. You can take steps to protect your financial security and your children while at the same time being cooperative and amicable with your spouse. You can rest assured that if your spouse has an attorney (and often even if he or she doesn't) he or she is taking similar defensive measures. Protecting yourself doesn't mean you have to be sneaky, mean, or money hungry. It does mean that you put yourself and your children first.

You're on your own now. You have to look out for yourself. You relied on your spouse in the past, but you can't do so anymore.

Dealing with Money

You probably have many different joint accounts with your spouse—bank accounts, credit cards, loans, and so on. The first step in protecting yourself is to make sure your spouse can't create financial problems for you.

Cash

Make sure you have some cash on hand. If your bank accounts and credit cards are frozen (which can happen if the judge decides to do so, or if your spouse freezes the credit cards), you will need money. Withdraw enough cash to get you through at least two weeks without using a credit card, debit card, or check. Keep it someplace safe and use it only in an emergency.

Bank Accounts

If you don't have a separate bank account in your own name, it's time to open one. You can do so with as little as one dollar. What's important is opening it, not how much you have in it. You need to establish your own credit and your own financial system.

Next you need to take a look at your joint checking and savings accounts. The best plan of action is to agree with your spouse to close these accounts and split the cash. Another choice is to keep one joint account functioning and use it to pay household expenses (for a jointly owned home) until the divorce is resolved. If you do this, you must agree how much each of you will deposit on a regular basis and you must trust that your spouse will not use this money for other things.

You both have the right to withdraw all the funds from a joint account at any time without the other's permission, whether it contains $10 or $10,000. If you are worried, take half of the money from the account and place it in a separate account. This way you will have access to your half no matter what. Your spouse's attorney may object, but if it is clear you have placed this money in an account for safekeeping and not with the intent to spend it all on yourself, it won't be a problem. Make sure you consult with your attorney before making any decisions about bank accounts. Your attorney can ask the judge to issue a temporary order determining who has access to which accounts or freezing certain accounts. While this is the safest course of action, it takes time; if you are worried about the money disappearing, withdrawing half may be the best solution in the short term.

Credit Cards

Either of you can charge anything to joint cards, and both of you will be held responsible by the credit card company. If your spouse refuses to pay or goes bankrupt, you're on the hook for the entire amount, even if you aren't the one who charged the item and even if you didn't know about it. If you use the card and don't pay the balance, your spouse can ask the court to order you to pay it. Either way, using joint cards complicates things and increases attorney fees.

Because of this joint liability, it's essential to close your joint accounts as soon as possible and open new accounts in your own name. If you have remaining balances on the joint cards, you can do one of two things: you can each transfer a portion of the debt to single accounts to pay off separately, or you can leave the account open but instruct the credit card company that no new charges can be made on it. The latter course of action freezes the account (and requires both of you to agree to unfreeze it) until the divorce settlement sorts out who will be responsible for it. Once the court decides this, you need to transfer the balance to solo accounts or pay it off immediately, because even if a court orders that your spouse is responsible for a joint account balance, that won't stop the credit card company from coming after you if payment is not made. Note also that even if the account is frozen, interest will continue to be charged to the account if the balance is not paid off.

If your divorce drags on for over a year, it may be a good idea to order your credit report every five or six months to make sure your spouse has not applied for a joint credit card or loan without your consent.

Credit Report

Get a copy of your credit report from all three credit reporting agencies:

Experian
888-397-3742
www.experian.com

Trans Union
P.O. Box 2000
Chester, PA 19022
800-916-8800
www.transunion.com

Equifax
P.O. Box 740241
Atlanta, GA 30374
800-685-1111
www.equifax.com

Your credit report will list all credit cards and loans in your name (including those that are joint). You can close accounts that are open but inactive to prevent future abuse by your spouse, and you'll find out if your spouse opened any new joint accounts without your knowledge. You'll also get your credit score and see if you are delinquent on any accounts.

You're not entitled to a copy of your spouse's report; only he or she can obtain that.

Joint Investments

As soon as you begin divorce proceedings, freeze all your joint investment accounts so nothing can be withdrawn from them and so loans can't be placed against them. As with cash, you could remove half and place it in an account for safekeeping, but it is best to discuss this strategy with your attorney.

Children's Accounts

If your children have bank accounts, investments, or college savings plans, they may be joint accounts with you or your spouse. If your spouse's name is on the accounts, there is nothing you can do on your own to prevent him or her from draining them. Get copies of the account statements and let your attorney know about the accounts so that he or she can ask the court to freeze them. If your name appears on the accounts, make sure you leave them intact during the divorce proceedings.

Retirement Accounts

If your spouse has a retirement account (including 401(k)s and IRAs) in his or her name, send a letter and ask the plan administrator for a copy of the brochure, plan, or summary as well as a current account statement. This way you have documentation of what is in the account and how the plan works. A retirement account (the portion of it accrued during the marriage) is something to be taken into consideration in a property settlement. You might want to take a cash settlement or have the right to collect a portion of the payments when your spouse retires. See Chapter 9 for more information about retirement accounts.

Safe-Deposit Boxes

If you have a joint safe-deposit box that holds cash or assets, ask the bank to require both signatures to open the box. Use the Safe-Deposit Box Inventory at the end of this chapter to create a record of everything in the box. Your other choice is to take out half of what's in the box to protect yourself. Consult with your attorney about this.

Bills

Your household bills may be joint or sole accounts. If they are joint and you move out of the home, make sure your name is removed from the account; otherwise you will continue to be responsible for them. You do not want to turn the utilities off if your spouse is still living in the home (this will be viewed as an unpleasant tactic by the court), but you do want to make sure you are no longer financially liable.

If the bills are in your spouse's name and he or she has moved out of the home, consider having the accounts transferred to your name so that your spouse cannot have the utilities turned off. Note, however, that doing so will make you completely responsible for paying the bill, whereas if it is in your spouse's name, he or she bears the responsibility. Discuss the implications of this issue with your attorney. It is possible that the court will order your spouse to pay these bills, so be sure to ask about this.

The Home

Physically separating can bring a lot of relief, but when and how to do so is an important strategic decision. If you move out and leave the children with the other parent, you are setting things up for him or her to have custody. Additionally, if you move out it decreases the chance that you will get possession of the home. For these reasons, it is a good idea to talk to your attorney before you decide to move out. Don't make the decision in a fit of anger.

Despite these caveats, there are times when living in the same house becomes unbearable and moving out is the only choice you have in the heat of the moment. If this happens, talk to your attorney as soon as possible to see what you can do to protect your rights after the fact. Try to wait until you can ask the court for a temporary order directing exclusive occupancy of the home to one of you.

If one of you does move out, you'll want to record this date on your master calendar.

Household Belongings

Use the Household Belongings Inventory at the end of the chapter to document and describe the more valuable objects you and your spouse own. Write down serial numbers for items that have them. Copy title and registration papers for cars driven by you and your spouse. Photograph or videotape all valuable items. Be sure the time and date stamp on the video camera and snapshot camera is enabled, because it provides you with concrete proof of the items' existence on the date you film them. Write a description on the back of each photograph. Store the photos in the "Household Inventory" pocket of your accordion file. Be sure to include:

- jewelry
- electronics (televisions, stereos, computers)
- vehicles
- valuable collections
- antiques
- other items worth over $500

Mail

Even if you are not moving, open a post office box in your name alone. You can request that your attorney and other professionals involved in the case send correspondence to you there. This way your spouse cannot access any of your mail and you don't have to worry that he or she will read it or take it. Even if you have physically separated, your mail is not necessarily secure. It is easy for mail to be removed from your home or roadside box without your knowledge. A P.O. box is a good idea if you have any concerns about security or privacy.

Home Security

Once your spouse has moved out and the court has given you sole occupancy, change the locks. He or she is still an owner of the home, but you have possession. Ask your attorney about getting a court order that gives you exclusive possession of the home, which will bolster your right to change the locks. Reset your home security system so that it takes a new code. Change the access code on your answering machine.

Change where you hide the spare key to the house. If there are any unsecured windows or doors, make sure they are repaired and secured. Ask that your spouse return garage door openers.

Passwords

Change passwords for ATM cards, online access to bank accounts, and online sites you shop at and have credit card information on file with. Change the password to any individual e-mail accounts you have, as well, so that your spouse cannot access them.

Keys

Request that your spouse return his or her keys to your car or vehicle, if the court has not already ordered him or her to do so. It's expensive to get the locks changed, so try your best to get the keys back. If he or she has a remote door opener for the vehicle, ask for that back, too. If you have an emergency key hidden somewhere on the vehicle, remove it or change where it is hidden.

If your spouse has keys to your parents' home or to that of another relative, ask for those back as well. If you have a home safe, give your spouse any items that belong to him or her from the safe and ask for the key back. If the safe uses a combination lock, contact the manufacturer for instructions on changing the code.

Insurance

Consider switching your auto insurance from a joint policy to a single policy. Since you will no longer be driving each other's cars, there's no reason to continue a joint policy. You will lose your multicar discount (if you have one) and will pay more, but you won't have to worry about the fact that if your spouse has an accident you will face an increase in your rate. If ownership of the cars is going to be in question, you may need to continue joint insurance to protect both of your interests until the court determines ownership.

If you have only one car, you will need a court order to determine who will keep it. Remember that even if the car is in only one spouse's name, the other spouse can be given possession of it because it is a marital asset. If you are given possession of the car, make sure you are listed as an authorized driver with the insurance company. If you are not, ask your spouse to change this. If he or she refuses, your attorney should ask the court to order him or her to do so. When your divorce is finalized, permanent ownership will be decided. If you get the car at that point, title will be transferred to you and you will need to obtain your own insurance policy.

If your spouse is your life insurance beneficiary, contact your agent and complete a change of beneficiary form.

If you have moved out of the home, keep your name on the home owner's insurance policy until the court makes a final decision about ownership. You're still an owner of the home and you want to protect that investment. If you and your spouse were renters and you move out of the residence, make sure the renter's insurance is kept in force as a joint policy, thus protecting any items that are yours or that will be yours after the divorce is settled. If you move out of the home and become a renter, make sure you obtain a renter's policy for your new residence.

Wills

While you might want to change your will to cut out your spouse, you need to wait until after the divorce to do so. If you disinherit your spouse in your will and die before the divorce is final, in most states the spouse is allowed to get a share of your estate despite what you wrote in your will. It is a good idea, though, to obtain a copy of your will and to make an appointment with your attorney to change it after your divorce. You'll also want to think about guardianship for your children. In most cases, the children would live with the other parent if you die, but if you want to avoid this, you'll need a guardianship clause in your will. See Chapter 17 for more information about this topic.

Powers of Attorney

If you have executed any powers of attorney giving your spouse authority to handle financial or business affairs on your behalf, destroy them, renege them in writing, or create a new one that supersedes the old one. Send a copy of the new form to any company or person who has one on file. Since power of attorney forms vary by state, check with your attorney to be sure you are using the proper form.

Health Care Directives

Sometimes called health care powers of attorney, living wills, or health care proxies, health care directives are documents that give another person the authority to make health care decisions for you should you ever be in a situation where you are unable to make your own decisions. You need to destroy or amend those that list your spouse as the person having this authority on your behalf. Talk to your attorney about the required form in your state, and make sure you send copies of the new document to your doctors or any other health care provider that has a copy of your old form.

Your Physical Safety

If you have been physically abused or threatened by your spouse, or fear that he or she will abuse you, you first need to protect your physical safety and then worry about assets and belongings. If you are in danger, get to a domestic violence shelter immediately. If you don't feel you are in immediate danger, ask your attorney about obtaining an order of protection or a restraining order against your spouse. Keep the phone number for your closest domestic violence shelter handy, and remember that you should always call 911 first if you are in danger, because you will get an immediate response and protection from the local police.

Protecting Your Children

If your children have been abused by your spouse, call your state's child abuse hotline (usually located in the front of your phone book). If you can't find the number, get it from your local police. If your children are in immediate danger, you need to get them out of harm's way first and worry about possessions and belongings later. Contact your local domestic violence shelter or your local department of social services or child and family services for information about what to do and where to go.

If you are concerned about parental kidnapping, talk to your attorney and get a temporary order of custody. Then notify all schools and child care providers that your child is to be released only to you. Give them a copy of the court order. Get a passport for your child and keep it in a safe-deposit box. Only one passport can be issued per person, and without it your child cannot be legally taken out of the country. Keep recent photos and fingerprints of your children in case they are ever needed (state police can provide home fingerprint kits, or you can go to their barracks and have it done).

Use the Self-Protection Checklist at the end of this chapter to make sure you have taken all necessary steps to protect yourself and your children.

Pets

Pets are considered to be another type of household possession, even though for many people they are like children. If there is a dispute over where your pets will live, you can get a temporary order from the court deciding where they will stay. If you are worried about your pets' safety, keep them in the house with you when you can't be outside to supervise them.

SAFE-DEPOSIT BOX INVENTORY

Box # _____

Financial Institution _____

Contents as of _____ (date)

_____

_____

_____

_____

_____

_____

_____

_____

_____

_____

_____

_____

_____

_____

_____

_____

_____

_____

_____

_____

_____

_____

_____

HOUSEHOLD BELONGINGS INVENTORY

Description and Serial Number	Location	Approximate Value

SELF-PROTECTION CHECKLIST

- ☐ Keep cash on hand.
- ☐ Withdraw from or protect bank accounts.
- ☐ Close or freeze joint credit cards.
- ☐ Obtain credit report.
- ☐ Obtain a P.O. box.
- ☐ Secure your home (change security code, make sure all windows and doors lock, change hidden key, change locks).
- ☐ Change passwords for e-mail and online accounts.
- ☐ Obtain extra keys from your spouse for cars, relatives' homes, and garage door openers.
- ☐ Change auto insurance.
- ☐ Change your life insurance beneficiary.
- ☐ Maintain home owner's or renter's insurance.
- ☐ Obtain copy of your will.
- ☐ Change powers of attorney.
- ☐ Change health care directives.
- ☐ Evaluate your physical safety and the safety of your children.
- ☐ Take steps to ensure pets' safety.

3

Working with an Attorney
and Other Professionals

If you don't already have an attorney, it is important that you get one as soon as you (or your spouse) decide that you are going to get a divorce. If you are on the fence about a divorce, an attorney can help you understand the process, the costs, and the possible outcomes. Some divorces can be handled without an attorney, but in a contested divorce (one in which your spouse has an attorney and you are not going to agree to everything he or she asks for) you will be best served to hire an attorney.

The legal profession has a bad reputation, but you need an attorney to protect yourself in a divorce. Most attorneys are honest and hardworking, but if you feel they are generally untrustworthy, you need to work extra hard to find one you can trust. You're going to spend a lot of time with this person and rely on him or her for important advice, so be choosy.

Finding an Attorney

If you have used an attorney in the past for speeding tickets or real estate, you might ask him or her for a referral to an attorney whose practice focuses on divorce. It is important to use an attorney who is experienced in handling divorces. You wouldn't hire your family doctor to operate on your heart even though he or she might know something about cardiac surgery. You want an expert—someone who knows all the tricks of the trade and has a lot of experience in that area.

Referrals are a great way of finding someone with whom you can build a good working relationship. Ask friends and relatives for suggestions, or call your city, county, or state bar association. Most have programs that will refer you to an experienced divorce attorney in your area. The American Academy of Matrimonial Lawyers (www.aaml.org or 312-263-6477) can also provide referrals. Once you have the name of an attorney, you can get some basic information about him or her by calling your state bar association or by looking in the Martindale-Hubbell directory (available at libraries in book format or online at www.martindale.com).

Questions to Ask an Attorney

Once you have a referral to an attorney, schedule a free consultation. You can't be charged for anything until you agree to a fee. Go into the office and interview the attorney. Don't be intimidated. Before you purchase a new car, you ask a lot of questions and take it for a test drive. Why should this be any different? The following questions can help you determine if the attorney is someone you want to handle your divorce.

Questions to Ask Yourself
- Do you feel comfortable in the waiting room?
- Are the office personnel friendly and polite?
- Does the office appear organized?
- Are you kept waiting longer than you are comfortable with?
- Does the office seem frantic or calm?
- Is parking nearby and convenient?
- Is the office convenient to get to from your home or workplace?

Questions to Ask the Attorney
- *Where did you go to law school?* The answer isn't terribly important, but if he or she went to a school overseas or to one you've never heard of, you should be wary.
- *How long have you been practicing this type of law?* Look for an attorney who has been practicing at least several years.

- *How many divorce cases have you handled in the past six months?* Look for an attorney who has handled at least ten in the last six months.
- *What are your fees?* Find out what the attorney charges for expenses such as copying.
- *What is your hourly rate?* Fees vary across the country, but you should expect to be charged $100 an hour and up. The more experienced the attorney, the higher the fee.
- *Is there a retainer fee?* A retainer fee is like a down payment you make when you agree to hire the attorney. Expect there to be one, but make sure it is an amount you can afford.
- *How much are the court fees?* Court fees will vary from state to state. If you have concerns about the fees you are quoted, call your local bar association for confirmation.
- *Can I get my spouse to pay the court fees and part or all of the attorney fees?* This will depend on your situation, but the attorney can give you an educated guess.
- *Can you estimate a total cost for my case?* The attorney should be able to give you a ballpark figure. Don't be surprised if your case costs over $10,000.
- *Will I receive a written contract for your services?* The contract might also be called a retainer agreement or a retainer letter. Make sure you work with an attorney who will provide one.
- *What expenses am I responsible for?* Find out what office expenses are not included in the hourly rate.
- *How often will I be billed?* Most attorneys will bill monthly.
- *Can a payment plan be worked out?* Some attorneys are willing to do this, so if you need a flexible payment schedule, keep looking until you find one.
- *Will you personally be handling my case?* If not, ask to meet the person who will be, and make sure one person is in charge of your case.
- *How long do you estimate the case will take?* The attorney should be able to estimate when the case will be concluded.
- *Do you feel I have a good chance to get what I want?* Try to get a feeling for how this attorney views your chances.
- *What am I asking for that I might not get?* This question will require the attorney to be specific. Even if the news is bad, it is important to know it now.

- *Do you plan on trying to settle this case?* Most attorneys will engage in settlement negotiations. Settlement is always cheaper than trial from your perspective.
- *How long does it take you to return phone calls?* You want an attorney who will return calls within twenty-four hours.
- *Who can I reach if there is a problem after hours?* It is rare to find an attorney who has a twenty-four-hour emergency line, but it is still a good idea to ask.
- *Is there someone available to handle emergencies if you are unavailable?* This can be a paralegal or another attorney.

Think about the answers you got and evaluate whether this is someone you feel comfortable with.

Understanding What Your Attorney Needs from You

Your attorney cannot manage your case without your help. Because divorces deal primarily with financial and custody matters, you need to provide your attorney with all of the information he or she requests, including records of finances, expenses, debts, and property. Expect to be asked to divulge personal information, such as the reason for your divorce, financial information, and things that will support your custody position (information on your lifestyle and parenting abilities). You have all the facts in the case, and it is your job to convey them to your attorney accurately and in a form that is easy to access so that he or she can input the information into court documents. This will make your case easy for the attorney to prepare and present.

Many clients are not completely honest with their divorce attorneys. They don't supply needed documents, or they leave out important pieces of information, especially anything that makes them look bad. You may resent having to give out private information, but it is all for your benefit. Your attorney is there to help you. You are a team, so make sure you are honest with your attorney.

Be a client who is calm, coherent, and reasonable. Attorneys spend a lot of time calming clients down and listening to their personal feelings, despite the fact that they are not trained to do this. Your attorney will handle the legal aspect of your divorce, but he or she is not trained to help you cope with the

30

emotional aspect. Therapists cost much less per hour than attorneys, so see one if you need to, instead of paying your attorney to listen.

Be a client who can follow instructions. When your attorney asks you to provide information, he or she is asking because the information is necessary. If you don't understand a request, ask for clarification. Try to follow all of the requests and advice as best you can. You will save money if your attorney does not have to spend additional time helping you get the information together.

Let your attorney know you have purchased this book, and give him or her copies of all the lists, logs, and documents you create. Take this book and your accordion file with you to every meeting you have with your attorney and to every court appearance. Keep them in a convenient place at home so that if you have a phone call with your attorney, you have the information at hand.

Do not share this book with your spouse! It will help you work on strategy and documentation. No matter how friendly your relationship is, you need to play some cards close to the vest.

Working with Your Attorney

Working with an attorney takes some patience. You have to remember that he or she has other responsibilities. While your case is important, there might be others that are more pressing at certain times. This doesn't mean that your questions or concerns should be ignored, though.

It's up to you to convey the seriousness of your concerns, but if you call twice a week with a "pressing" concern, your attorney isn't going to be very fast to respond. It's important to be patient with your attorney, but you also need to know when to stand up and say "I need something right now"—a careful balancing act at times. You don't want to involve your attorney in every disagreement you have with your spouse or every conflict that occurs with visitation. You do, however, want to let your attorney know when major crises develop. Don't be timid when you need advice or information. If you do not get a timely response from your attorney when you need something, call again and leave a detailed message.

If your attorney has a legal secretary or paralegal, you can try to speak to him or her. Although these professionals generally are not able to give you advice, they may be able to reach the attorney to get an answer to your question or problem.

Time is money when it comes to attorneys. The more time you spend with your attorney, the more it's going to cost you. That's why it is important to approach meetings or phone calls in an organized way. Think about your questions or issues in advance, and list them on the Questions and Issues to Discuss with Your Attorney worksheet at the end of this chapter. Take notes on everything your attorney tells you, especially when on the phone; afterward, make notes in answer to your questions. You may have a good memory, but there are so many emotional issues involved that you won't always be thinking clearly. If you take clear notes, you can return to them later to refresh your memory, to back up what the attorney has told you, or to clarify information you've provided. It's almost impossible to ask all your questions in the first meeting with your attorney. You will forget things, and new questions will arise after the meeting, which is to be expected. Remember one of the rules from Chapter 1: don't be too hard on yourself.

Ways to Avoid Time and Money Busters
- Call only when you have something important to discuss. Don't call just for an update. When there's something to report, your attorney will tell you.
- Present documents and papers in an orderly way. If you give your attorney a disorganized heap of papers, you're going to pay for someone in the office to straighten it out.
- Keep copies of all documents in case your lawyer cannot find something.
- Talk to a secretary or paralegal whenever possible instead of the attorney. These other professionals bill at a lower hourly rate.
- When you meet with your attorney, keep chitchat to a minimum. Remember, you are paying for that time.
- Try to work out informal agreements with your spouse about custody, visitation, and property and debt division. Your attorney can then formalize these decisions for you. Anything you can decide on your own will reduce your legal bills.
- Work with a mediator to settle unresolved issues. Most mediators bill at a lower hourly rate than attorneys, and both you and your spouse are receiving services at that lower rate. See Chapter 6 and later in this chapter for more information about mediation.
- Don't come to an appointment if you haven't gathered the necessary documents. Reschedule the meeting for a time when you will have the information at hand.

- Read a book or consult the Internet to answer your most basic questions about divorce law in your state so you don't need to take your attorney's time.
- Don't hide problems or important issues. They will almost always come back to bite you later, causing bigger problems and more legal bills than they would have if they had been dealt with up front. Be honest with your attorney, even if you aren't honest with anyone else.

Organizing Paperwork from Your Attorney

In the course of your case, you will receive several kinds of documents from your attorney. Some will be informational, like pamphlets and statements of your rights. Others will require you to fill in information and return them. Still others will be copies of court papers and correspondence that you should keep in chronological order by issue date. Store the documents you need to fill in and return, as well as the ones you need to keep, in your accordion file.

Phone Calls with Professionals

You'll probably have many phone calls with your attorney and other professionals involved in your case. Use the Phone Call Log at the end of this chapter to keep notes about these calls. Write down appointments, instructions, or other information you are given.

A phone call log can be helpful if you are having difficulty getting in touch with your attorney. Make a note each time you leave him or her a message. If you've left several messages with no response, you can call back and say, "I left messages on the twelfth, thirteenth, fourteenth, and fifteenth but have not heard back yet."

Paying Your Attorney

You will receive bills from your attorney, as well as receipts for retainer fees and court fees that you've paid up front. Like any other office, an attorney's office can make billing mistakes, so check your invoices for accuracy. Make sure you record payments you make in your checkbook; if you pay with cash or money order, always ask for a receipt.

While some attorneys are willing to make allowances for clients who don't pay on time, others may drop you as a client, charge you interest, or begin collection proceedings against you if you don't pay.

Affording Your Attorney

Make sure that you know up front how much your divorce is going to cost you. Get a clear estimate from your attorney during your initial consultation. Ask if he or she will agree to payment plans. You'll find that in the beginning your monthly legal bill will be small, but once you are in the trial phase it can be quite large. Costs are more manageable if they are spread into equal payments over several months.

If you don't have the funds to pay your legal bills, think about borrowing money from family or friends. This is one of those times when you've got to call in favors. Many divorce clients end up paying their legal bills this way. If you have a very low income and very few assets, contact a legal aid clinic to find out if you qualify for free or reduced-fee legal assistance. Your local bar association can give you the number.

If your spouse has a higher income than you do, the court may direct him or her to pay your legal bills. Talk to your attorney about this possibility at your initial meeting.

Other Professionals Who May Be Involved with Your Case

Your attorney is probably the most important professional you will be dealing with throughout the divorce process, but other people may become involved in your case. Keep a detailed contact list so you can easily access these professionals when you need them. Use the Master List of Contact Information at the end of this chapter to record the phone numbers and addresses of these professionals.

Guardian ad Litem/Law Guardian

The court may appoint a law guardian, or guardian ad litem, to represent your child or children in the custody part of the case. This is an attorney who represents the children's point of view about custody and visitation to the court. Law guardians are often paid by the state, but in some instances the parents are required to pay the fees.

These attorneys are specially trained and are skilled at meeting children and understanding custody issues. The law guardian will probably contact you at the beginning of the case and may ask to set up a home visit. During the visit he or she will talk with you about your relationship with your child and your point of view about custody. He or she may also ask to speak privately with your child.

While it is a good idea to ask your attorney how to deal with the law guardian, it is usually in your best interest to be friendly and cooperative. In some states the law guardian makes a recommendation to the judge about custody and is very influential. You want him or her to be on your side.

Keep any correspondence from the law guardian in the accordion folder.

Appraiser

You may need to hire an appraiser to value your home, business, or other assets. Appraisers provide an estimated value of an asset so that the court has a number to work from when creating a property settlement. Be sure to select one who has experience with the type of asset you need valued. Your attorney will hire the appraiser but may ask for your input. Since you're paying, you can say you want the right of approval. In some cases, both spouses may hire appraisers and the court may request a third. It is usually in your best interest to help the appraiser reach an accurate valuation. If the asset you are given is not really worth what it is appraised at, you have lost out on tangible value. For example, suppose you are awarded an RV that is appraised at $50,000 while your spouse is given investments worth $50,000. Unfortunately, you can't get anyone to buy the RV for $50,000 because it is really worth only $30,000. That means you've just lost $20,000. Conversely, if an appraiser undervalues an asset and it goes to your spouse, your spouse ends up with a higher value than the court intended.

Keep all copies of reports and bills from appraisers in the accordion file.

35

Counselor/Therapist

A large number of families participate in counseling as part of the divorce process. Counseling can be helpful for you and your child. Counselors can suggest coping mechanisms to help you and your children through the rocky times of a divorce. They offer a place for you to talk freely without fear of repercussion.

To find a counselor:

- Ask your family doctor or pediatrician for a referral.
- Check the list of counselors who participate in your insurance plan.
- Ask family and friends for the names of counselors they have used.

Once you've found a counselor, you'll want to ask him or her the following questions:

- How experienced are you with children?
- How long have you been in practice?
- How experienced are you with issues of divorce?
- How much will the sessions cost?
- Are you available by phone if emergencies come up?
- What is the hourly rate?

In the course of a custody case you might be required to see a counselor, therapist, or psychologist for an evaluation. This professional is not there to help you work through problems, but to provide the court with an opinion about each parent's abilities and about the family dynamics. You won't gain anything by being uncooperative. Talk with your attorney if you are concerned about how to approach these evaluations.

Caseworker

If an allegation of child abuse is made, state caseworkers may be called in to investigate the allegations. If an investigation is begun, notify your attorney as soon as you know about it. Keep any pertinent documents in the accordion file and share them with your attorney.

Financial Advisor

If you have a financial advisor, you may need to contact him or her to obtain documents about your investments. Once you are divorced, it is a good idea to see separate financial planners to avoid any conflict or mistrust.

Accountant or Divorce Planner

Some attorneys routinely use accountants to help them plan a divorce settlement. If your case involves a closely held business or other complicated finances, an accountant can help untangle all the information. A certified divorce planner is a specially trained financial expert who will help you reach a settlement and explain the ramifications of financial decisions during divorce.

When working with an accountant or divorce planner, you need to consider your financial position. If you own a business and want the value minimized, you won't be as forthcoming with information as you would if you were the nonowner spouse. Discuss the possibilities with your attorney.

Retain all documents and bills from these professionals.

Mediator

A mediator is a neutral party who helps people reach a mutually acceptable settlement. Some states require that divorcing couples try mediation before heading to court. A mediator does not represent either you or your spouse, but works for both of you. You and your spouse need to have separate attorneys during mediation to explain what your options are. The attorneys also approve the settlement and then take it to court to finalize it. To make mediation work, you must approach it with a willing attitude and some faith in the process. Sometimes a mediator can help you resolve the issues involved in your divorce more quickly than an attorney can.

Collaborative Lawyers

Collaborative law is a new trend. Collaborative lawyers work with the spouses to reach a settlement. If you work with a collaborative lawyer and do not reach a settlement, you need to seek a new attorney to take your case to court.

QUESTIONS AND ISSUES TO DISCUSS WITH YOUR ATTORNEY

Make copies of this list for further use.

Date _____

Questions

_____

_____

_____

_____

_____

_____

_____

_____

_____

_____

Notes

_____

_____

_____

_____

_____

_____

_____

PHONE CALL LOG

Make copies of this log for further use.

Date	Time	Notes

MASTER LIST OF CONTACT INFORMATION

Make copies of this log for further use.

Name	Address	Business Phone	Cell Phone/Pager	E-Mail Address

4

Ways to End Your Marriage

While ending a marriage is never easy, you do have some choices to consider about the way to end your relationship.

Residency

Before you can file for divorce, you must meet your state's residency requirements. These are laws requiring you and/or your spouse to live in that state for a certain period of time before filing for divorce and can range from a few weeks to a year.

Grounds

The grounds for divorce—the legal reason why the marriage is being dissolved—place the blame on one spouse. Some states, such as California, have no-fault divorces. In these states you do not need to prove your spouse did something wrong in order to get a divorce. You simply say that you have irreconcilable differences, are incompatible, or have had an irretrievable breakdown in the relationship. Neither spouse needs to prove that this is true, and no evidence is presented to the court. Some states permit no-fault divorces only after you've been legally separated for a certain length of time.

In many other states, you must provide an acceptable reason for why you want a divorce. Reasons can include:

- *Abandonment.* Your spouse has left you or failed to support you.
- *Adultery.* Your spouse has had sexual intercourse with someone else during the marriage.
- *Cruel treatment.* Your spouse has treated you in a way that is mean or cruel (sometimes called cruel and inhuman, or cruel and inhumane, treatment).
- *Imprisonment.* Your spouse has been in prison during a portion of the marriage (there is normally a fixed minimum number of years to qualify) and must still be in prison when you file for the divorce.
- *Physical inability to have intercourse.* This ground can normally be used only if your spouse did not share this information with you prior to the marriage.

All of the grounds used by the plaintiff (the spouse requesting the divorce) relate to what the defendant (the other spouse) has done during the marriage. For example, you can't ask for a divorce because you've cheated on your spouse; you can only ask for a divorce because your spouse has cheated on you. A defendant can file a counterclaim asking the court to end the marriage because of something the plaintiff did. It's important to consult an attorney, because laws about grounds vary greatly and you must meet the exact requirements set out in your state law.

In states where grounds must be used, the couples generally agree on the grounds and the defendant consents to them. If there is no contest over the grounds, the plaintiff usually gives a short statement to the court about the facts that support the grounds, but there is no cross-examination, testimony from witnesses, or presentation of evidence. Most people agree that if their spouse wants a divorce, there is no point in dragging things out by making him or her prove the reasons for it.

Although it is rare to have a grounds trial, it does happen occasionally. This means that the defendant does not agree that he or she has done anything wrong and does not agree that there should be a divorce. Should this happen in your case, you will have a hearing just about the grounds. Your attorney will present evidence and testimony and your spouse's attorney will have the opportunity to cross-examine and present evidence and testimony to refute your case. The judge will decide whether or not there are adequate grounds to dissolve the marriage.

If you have to gather evidence for grounds, try to collect the following:

Abandonment
- proof that your spouse has taken a new residence, such as mail that has been delivered there or a phone book listing
- your recollections of conversations in which your spouse said he or she was leaving or of conversations in which your spouse refused your requests for financial support
- testimony from others about your spouse's intentions to leave

Imprisonment
- information about your spouse's conviction and sentence

Cruelty
- a written account of everything your spouse has done or said to you within the past two years that was cruel, painful, or dangerous (mentally, emotionally, or physically)
- names of others who have witnessed your spouse's behavior
- photographs and police reports documenting physical abuse by your spouse

Adultery
- testimony from private investigators or others who have witnessed the adultery firsthand
- photographs of the adultery

Physical Inability
- notes of attempts to consummate the marriage and the outcomes
- names of doctors who have been consulted

Annulment

An annulment is a decision by a court that the marriage was invalid at the time it occurred. Contrary to popular belief, it doesn't mean the marriage never happened. Any children born during the marriage are considered to be legitimate. A legal annulment is different from a religious annulment, which must be granted by a religious institution (a Jewish annulment is called a get).

Grounds for a legal annulment include:

- being underage at the time of the marriage
- misrepresenting yourself (saying, for example, that you are able to have children when you know you are unable to)
- being mentally ill
- being unable or unwilling to consummate the marriage (have intercourse)
- concealing important facts such as alcoholism or previous children

The criteria for annulment can vary greatly from state to state, so be sure to discuss this option with your attorney. Since most annulments are sought soon after the wedding, there is usually no need to divide property, decide custody, or award support or alimony. However, if your annulment does occur after a longer marriage, these issues will be decided by the court.

Legal Separation

44

A legal separation is a court order stating that you and your spouse are to live separate and apart. These orders usually specify everything else that a divorce judgment contains, such as child support, alimony, and property division, but they do not formally dissolve the marriage. In some states you can get a legal separation without going to court, simply by signing a separation agreement created by your attorney. The most common reason for seeking a separation is that in some states you can get a no-fault divorce after being separated for a certain period.

Don't confuse a legal separation with physical separation. When you and your spouse move to separate residences, you have physically separated, but you have not obtained a legal separation until you sign a document or the court issues an order declaring you separate.

Remaining Married

Some couples physically separate but never seek a legal separation or divorce. You are not required to divorce if you no longer want to live together—you can physically separate and go on with your lives. You will need to continue listing your marital status on income tax returns and other legal documents. Child support and custody can be determined by your state's family court. Complications arise if you have trouble dividing your assets and debts on your own. Some people are able to do so themselves, whereas others need to take the matter to court. It's important to note that if you never divorce, your spouse is entitled to inherit a portion of your estate if you die before him or her.

Ending a Common-Law Marriage

In some states, if you and a partner of the opposite sex live together and hold yourselves out as a married couple (by introducing each other as "my husband" or "my wife," filing a joint tax return, or using the title *Mrs.*, for example) your relationship becomes a legal marriage after a "significant period of time"—usually several years. If you meet the requirements of a common-law marriage in your state, then you will use your state's regular divorce procedure to end your marriage.

  If you do not meet your state's common-law marriage requirements, or if your state does not recognize common-law marriages, your marriage does not need to be legally dissolved. You can just physically separate. Custody and child support issues can be handled by your state's family court, but you will have to handle property and debt division on your own or in small-claims court. Talk to your attorney about this.

5

Step-by-Step Through Your Divorce

The divorce process and the entire court system can be intimidating, but it doesn't have to be. There is an order to the way things progress in your case, and understanding this can make you more comfortable with the process.

The System and the Way It Works

Because the court system is so foreign and the documents are usually written in confusing language, it's easy to feel as if you are in over your head. Once you understand what the court papers mean and how your case is going to proceed, you'll feel more organized and in control.

Initial Papers

Your divorce will begin with a petition, summons, or application for divorce filed by the plaintiff, the spouse who is bringing the case to court. The petition lists what the plaintiff is asking for and explains the reason for the divorce. If you're the plaintiff, you will have gone over this with your attorney prior to filing. If you're not, keep this document in a safe place because your attorney will need it. Store all of your court documents in your accordion folder.

After the petition (your state might call these initial papers by a different name) has been filed, the defendant has a chance to respond by filing an appearance, a response, or an answer. Then the plaintiff will file more papers that give additional details about the divorce. These papers may be served by a process server; if your attorney is in contact with your spouse's attorney, it can be arranged that service will be handled by the attorneys.

Initial Court Appearance

A date will be set for an initial appearance, when both parties in the case must come to court. Your attorney will send you a copy of the notice or call you with the information. Make sure you keep the notice and record the date on your calendar. The initial appearance can occur soon after the initial papers are filed if one of the parties is asking the court for a temporary order. A temporary order is a preliminary court order that decides certain issues on a temporary basis, such as where the children will live, whether child support will be paid, and who will remain in the marital residence while the case is pending. A short hearing may be held to decide about temporary orders.

If there are no requests for temporary orders, the initial appearance is usually a settlement conference, where the lawyers meet with someone from the judge's staff and try to reach a settlement. There may be several such pretrial conferences, and the court might suggest mediation as an alternative.

48

Discovery

The next stage of the process is discovery, when each side gathers information in preparation for the trial. You may have to produce documents or answer written questions (with the assistance of your lawyer). In hotly contested cases, depositions are sometimes taken. A deposition is sworn testimony that is given in an attorney's office and transcribed by a stenographer. The attorney uses this opportunity to ask the opposing party questions that will help him or her plan for the trial.

Trial

If your case does not settle, a trial will be scheduled. The trial is not usually completed in one day; it may be held in bits and pieces over several days.

When a trial is held, each side makes an opening statement, or brief summary of the case. Afterward, the plaintiff's attorney calls witnesses and presents evidence. The defendant has a chance to cross-examine those witnesses. Then the defendant presents witnesses and evidence and the plaintiff can cross-examine. The trial ends with closing statements in which each attorney states what he or she is asking for and how he or she wants the judge to rule.

The divorce will not be final until the judge's decision is rendered in writing. Most judges won't tell you what they've decided while you are in court. They make their decisions only in writing, and that can take several weeks. Once you get the decision, your attorney may have some paperwork to complete to finalize the divorce.

Appeals

An appeal asks a higher, more powerful court to review a decision made by the trial court. An appellate court reviews only issues of law, not issues of fact. It decides whether or not the trial court applied the law properly. The appellate court does not hear any new evidence or testimony, and there are no witnesses. It is purely a review of the legal decision made by the trial judge.

Appeals are most common at the end of the case—after the judge has issued a final judgment. However, your attorney can appeal temporary, initial, and interim orders and decisions at any point in the case.

If you feel that the decision made in your case is wrong or unfair, discuss it with your attorney. You have only a certain period of time to begin an appeal, and if you miss the window, there's nothing you can do.

If you decide to appeal, understand that it can be a lengthy process. You will not need to appear at any time. Your attorney will prepare a written brief, or argument, and send it to the appellate court. He or she may also appear in court to give an oral argument. Because the brief focuses completely on how the law was applied in your case, there is nothing you can do to assist your attorney in preparing it.

49

Court Papers

Throughout your divorce, your attorney will collect a huge stack of papers about your case, and you will receive copies of many of them. Keep them in a separate file with the most recent documents at the front. Then, if you need to double-check on a court date, you can easily find the most recent notice.

Your attorney will prepare all the documents you file in your case, and you will be required to sign them and swear that they are true. Because of this, it is important that you take the time to read them and make sure they are accurate before signing them. Double-check numbers on financial statements if they don't look right to you, and make sure the papers ask for everything you want to ask for.

Your attorney will also give you copies of some of the documents filed by your spouse. Read them carefully and point out things that are not true or that you do not agree with. Remember to save venting for friends and family. Use your time with your attorney to get down to business.

Here are some terms you might encounter when dealing with court papers:

Affiant: person signing an affidavit
Affidavit: a sworn written statement
Allegations: things a person claims to be true
Amend: to change a court paper
Answer: a paper filed by a defendant in response to the plaintiff's papers
Complaint: a form that lists specific reasons for divorce
Default: to not appear in court or to fail to respond to court papers
Docket number: case number
Ex parte: without the other party present; sometimes a judge will make an emergency decision with only one party in the courtroom
Jurisdiction: a court's ability to hear certain cases
Litigants: parties involved in the case (plaintiff and defendant)
Motion: a formal way of asking the court to decide something
Notary: licensed official who verifies signatures on papers
Pleadings: initial court papers
Pro se: without an attorney
Stipulation: an agreement or settlement

Most legal papers are sprinkled with legalese—words like "witnesseth," "hereby," "adjudged," "decreed," "therefore," "in accordance with," "pursuant," and so on. These words are often just formalities without much meaning. Don't get bogged down by the language. You don't need to know the exact definition of each word; you just need a sense of what the document says. If there is something substantial you don't understand, ask your attorney.

Appearing in Court

Going into court to have your divorce decided can be a momentous and stressful occasion. Most people have only been in court for things like traffic tickets or jury duty. If you know what to expect in advance and you arrive prepared, you can go to court feeling if not confident, at least organized and knowledgeable. Remember that very few people other than lawyers feel completely at ease in court. Judges and court personnel understand how you feel and often go out of their way to make you feel comfortable.

How to Dress

People are often judged by their appearance. When you go to court, it is important that you dress neatly and seriously. Avoid clothes and accessories that look flashy or too casual. These include:

- hats
- bare legs (even in the summer with a dress)
- open-toed shoes
- sandals
- a lot of jewelry, no matter how tasteful
- large jewelry (real or fake)
- loud or flashy clothing
- ripped or torn clothing
- big hair
- facial stubble
- T-shirts
- shorts
- jeans
- tight or revealing clothing

- tattoos
- excessive makeup
- very long nails
- wrinkled or stained clothing
- sunglasses
- work boots
- flannel shirts
- body piercing (other than ears)
- short skirts
- sneakers
- stiletto heels

The preferred attire for men is a suit or a sport coat and tie. A sweater or a shirt with a collar would also be appropriate. The preferred attire for women is a suit or a dress. A pantsuit, a skirt and blouse, or pants and a sweater are also acceptable.

When deciding what to wear, keep in mind that you want to look:

- respectable
- serious
- conservative
- responsible
- reliable
- trustworthy
- dependable
- financially modest
- friendly

Certainly, you are who you are, but when you go to court you aren't there to make a political or fashion statement. You're there to win over the judge and get what you want. This means you've got to play by the judge's rules. Judges like litigants who dress conservatively, act appropriately, and look like upstanding citizens.

Since you will probably have to go to court several times, assemble a few outfits in advance to choose from. This way you won't panic the morning of your hearing. Always have a backup outfit in case something is wrong with the one you choose.

Understanding Courtroom Procedures

Everyone has seen courtrooms—either on reality TV or on drama shows. For the most part, real courtrooms are similar to TV courtrooms.

The Courtroom

Some courtrooms are huge, formal places. Others are small, plain rooms, sometimes in temporary buildings or annexes. Ask your attorney where your courtroom is and how to get there. Ask what kind of room it is and where you should meet.

The judge will sit behind a bench that may be raised or at eye level. There will usually be at least two or three tables for the parties and their attorneys. Generally, the plaintiff sits on the right and the defendant on the left, but this can vary according to custom or judge. Sit where your attorney tells you.

Many courtrooms are open to the public, which means that people can come in (including the media) and observe the case. Unless your case is high profile, it is unlikely that anyone will observe your case. If this is something you are worried about, talk to your attorney.

Court Personnel

When you enter the courthouse, you will probably first encounter security personnel. They may ask you to step through a metal detector and may x-ray or search your belongings. Note that weapons and sharp objects are not permitted in courthouses.

You may next encounter a court clerk. If there is a waiting room, you will need to check in and let the clerk know you are there. A bailiff usually calls the cases. Bailiffs usually wear uniforms and keep order in the courtroom.

Inside the courtroom there will be a court stenographer who transcribes everything that is said during the proceedings. Some cases are tape-recorded rather than transcribed on-site. There may also be a court clerk or secretary inside the courtroom to assist the judge with scheduling and paperwork.

When you go to court initially, you might not appear in front of a judge. You might instead be meeting with a matrimonial referee, law clerk, hearing officer, or some other quasi-judicial person. Ask your lawyer in advance who is presiding. Whoever presides over your case is acting in an official capacity and must be treated with respect. Judges should be referred to as "Your Honor." Other personnel can be referred to as "Sir" or "Ma'am."

Courtroom Manners

If you are represented by an attorney, you shouldn't need to do a lot of talking when in the courtroom. In general, you should talk only when:

- the judge asks you a question
- your lawyer asks you a question
- you have something urgent or important you need to tell your attorney
- you are on the witness stand

Don't talk to your spouse or your spouse's attorney while in the courtroom (unless he or she is questioning you), and never interrupt when the judge is speaking.

When you are in the courtroom, you must stand whenever the judge does so (usually when he or she is entering or exiting the courtroom). You will be asked to stand when the judge is making a decision or issuing an order.

What to Bring to Court

You can rely on your attorney to handle the paperwork involved in your divorce, but no one is infallible. Thus, it's always best to come to court prepared. Assume your attorney will have everything, but bring all of your documents along just in case. That includes financial affidavits and statements, pay stubs, your calendar, and temporary or previous court orders. Bring this book and your accordion file with you. If you have used it well, you will have everything you could possibly need at your fingertips.

It is also a good idea to bring along a notepad and a pen in case you want to write your attorney a note in court or jot down things to ask about later (it's usually OK to lean over and whisper to your attorney).

Find out in advance how long you can expect to be at court. If it is an all-day trial, do a little research before you go looking for a place nearby to have lunch. Your attorney might have lunch with you, or he or she may need to go back to the office during the break.

Some people like to bring along a friend or relative for support. If you do, he or she will not sit at your table and may even be asked to wait in the hall. Do not turn to look at or talk to your companion during court proceedings.

Do not bring food, beverages, or gum into the courtroom. Most large courthouses have food vendors or vending machines you can use during breaks.

What Can Happen in Court

What can happen in court depends on what you are scheduled for. Initial appearances can include arguments about temporary orders as well as short hearings (where you may need to testify) to determine how the judge will rule on temporary requests. A judge can issue new or altered temporary orders at any appearance.

Once the temporary orders are in place, court appearances are usually for settlement purposes. The attorneys generally meet in private with court personnel to discuss possible settlements. Your attorney may come out to talk over possible compromises with you and then go back into the meeting.

When you go to court for hearings and trial, the atmosphere will be more formal and procedural. The plaintiff calls witnesses and the defense gets to cross-examine them. Once the plaintiff has called all witnesses and presented all of his or her documentary evidence, the defense presents its case and the plaintiff cross-examines. In many states, if custody is an issue, a guardian ad litem, or law guardian, is appointed to represent the children. The law guardian can cross-examine all witnesses called in the custody phase of the trial and can present his or her own witnesses as well.

The Unexpected

If something is said in court that is not true and you believe your attorney is not aware of it, make a point of letting him or her know. If your attorney has some facts or dates wrong, don't be afraid to point it out, but do so quietly by whispering or writing.

If you become overwrought with anger or sadness, ask your attorney to request a break to get yourself together. Everyone involved in the case understands how emotional it is.

Avoid any direct conflict with your spouse. Your attorneys will probably make sure this doesn't happen, but if your spouse tries to start an argument with you in the hall or waiting room, move away. If that doesn't help, call for security.

If you get to court and your attorney is not there, don't panic. Attorneys often have other cases scheduled at the same time. If your case is called and he or she has not yet appeared, let the bailiff or court clerk know. The court will either call the attorney or postpone the appearance. Do not proceed without your attorney. Note that if your attorney is consistently late or frequently misses court appearances, you may need to discuss the problem with him or her.

6

Settlement Options

Most divorces end up settling. A settlement is usually the most desirable way to end a divorce since both parties walk away feeling that they have won in some way. It also avoids the need for hurtful testimony and expensive trials. A settlement allows you to work out an agreement that is best for both of you (and your children). Although judges try to make decisions that are fair, they don't know your situation as well as you do and can't possibly understand everything involved in the divorce. Creating a settlement gives you control over the situation and allows you to tailor an agreement that fits your situation. There are several paths you can take to get to a settlement.

Mediation

Mediation is a process in which both parties in the divorce meet with a mediator who acts as a neutral third party. The mediator helps the divorcing couple explore their settlement options and encourages them to create a settlement that fits their personal needs. The mediator works for both the husband and the wife, remaining completely neutral. He or she does not make decisions for the couple but helps them find the solutions themselves.

In some states, mediation is mandatory—you have to try it before you can continue through the court process. In most states, though, it is still a relatively untraveled path.

The Benefits of Mediation

Mediation offers many benefits to a couple. The process teaches conflict-resolution skills, so the parties emerge with new skills to help them resolve problems that may arise in the future with regard to parental access or finances. Additionally, mediation allows couples to take charge of their situation. Going to court and having a judge decide your fate can be a very passive experience. By engaging in mediation, a couple takes the reins and actively searches for solutions. The solutions found in mediation are often customized to fit that couple's particular needs and are far more detailed than the directives most courts would provide. And because they help create the settlements, couples are more likely to adhere to them. Mediated settlements also provide closure in ways court decisions can't. You and your spouse work through a defined process that is very personal, and together you create an agreement that resolves your problems. In most cases, participants walk away feeling satisfied and relieved. Mediation ends up being less expensive than a contested divorce and allows the couple to avoid a lot of the anger that accompanies a traditional divorce. The focus is on solutions, not problems.

Mediation also is a great benefit for the children in a divorce. Instead of having their parents at each other's throats, dragging each other into court, the parents work together to decide how they will parent their children in the future. This creates a cooperative atmosphere that truly benefits the children. Some mediators even invite older children into the sessions so their opinions are heard. Mediation provides a good conflict-resolution model for kids. They see that the best way to solve problems is by talking about them and compromising.

Deciding if Mediation Is for You

To decide if mediation is right for you, ask yourself these questions:

- Are you fearful for your physical safety?
- Does your spouse refuse to listen to you?
- Do you have a hard time standing up for what you want?
- Are you uncomfortable sitting in the same room with your spouse?
- Is your spouse unwilling to try to compromise?
- Would you be happier having an attorney handle all decisions for you?

- Do you have trouble expressing what you want or talking about the divorce without getting upset?
- Are you really out for revenge?

If you answered yes to most of these questions, mediation may not work for you. If you are unsure, talk to your attorney.

Choosing a Mediator

If you think mediation is something you and your spouse should at least consider, set up a free consultation appointment with an area mediator. If you already have a matrimonial attorney, ask him or her for a referral. Some attorneys are resistant to mediation because they see it as taking work away from them, but a matrimonial attorney should be in favor of anything that reduces conflict and benefits the client. Don't let your attorney talk you out of mediation if it is something you would like to try.

To find a mediator, you can contact your local bar association's referral program or check the list of resources in the Appendix at the end of this book. Many states have mediation associations that can refer you to a mediator in your area.

The mediator will want to meet with both you and your spouse. Since he or she must remain neutral, meeting with either of you alone would be unethical.

In most states there is no licensing of mediators. You do not need any education, training, or approval to become a mediator. However, most mediators are attorneys or therapists who do mediation in addition to their professional practice. Mediation has ties to both of these professions, so you can usually feel comfortable with mediators who are lawyers or therapists. If your state does license mediators, be sure to seek out one who is licensed.

Questions to Ask a Mediator
- How long have you done mediation?
- What are your qualifications?
- How long does the average case take to resolve?
- How often do you meet with a couple?
- Are fees charged hourly?
- What is your hourly rate?

- Is there a retainer?
- What kind of agreement do you prepare at the end of the mediation program?

Questions to Ask Yourself
- Did you feel comfortable in the office?
- Is the mediator someone you can trust and feel comfortable with?
- Are you comfortable with the process of mediation as the mediator explained it?
- Will you be able to be honest and open during mediation?
- Do you trust your spouse to be honest and offer full financial disclosure during mediation?

The Mediation Process

Most divorces can be settled in seven to ten mediation sessions. When you agree to work with a mediator, you will sign an agreement that outlines the fee arrangement (usually a retainer with an hourly rate), the mediator's responsibilities, and your responsibilities. Because mediation is meant to be a safe place, couples with a history of domestic violence are not candidates for mediation, and most mediators set rules for how the spouses may treat each other during the sessions, emphasizing respect and restraint.

The mediator usually emphasizes that he or she is only a guide and that the couple must do the actual work of finding a settlement. The mediator can provide legal information but cannot give either party personal legal advice. For this reason, both spouses must have separate attorneys to consult throughout the process. The attorneys will also review the agreement that is reached.

Both spouses must agree to make full financial disclosure to each other during mediation, as they would in court. This means you have to provide each other with complete information about your assets and debts.

Once the mediation process has ended, the mediator will prepare a document laying out the terms of the settlement agreement. One spouse's attorney will then take the settlement to court.

You can make mediation successful by:

- keeping all appointments
- taking time to think through all important issues

- avoiding knee-jerk reactions when possible
- trying not to push your spouse's buttons
- making decisions about custody based on what is best for your children
- doing any homework your mediator assigns
- providing full financial disclosure
- offering alternatives and creative solutions
- being honest about your preferences
- talking to your attorney about your settlement options in court before you mediate
- choosing a mediator you are comfortable with
- deciding at the beginning how you and your spouse will pay for mediation (whether you will split the cost or one of you will pay for it completely)
- staying focused on the big picture and not getting hung up on small decisions

Arbitration

Arbitration is usually thought of as an alternative to court for cases such as labor disputes. In those cases, parties can have their case decided by an arbitrator in much the same way a judge would decide the case. Arbitration for matrimonial cases is still a rarity, but there are pilot programs in some areas. In these programs, cases are sent to a neutral evaluator (usually an experienced attorney) who evaluates them with both attorneys present and offers an opinion on how a judge would decide. The parties and their attorneys use this information to come to a settlement. If you're interested in arbitration, ask your attorney if this type of program is available in your area.

Collaborative Law

Collaborative law, discussed in Chapter 3, is a fairly new field that is becoming increasingly popular. In collaborative law, each party hires an attorney who specializes in that field, and the attorneys work together to reach a settlement.

Reaching a settlement is their only goal. This process works well for spouses who prefer a mediation-like approach but don't want to negotiate for themselves. If a settlement cannot be reached using the collaborative law process, the parties must find new attorneys who will handle the court case because a collaborative lawyer does not handle contested cases in court.

To find a collaborative lawyer, contact your local or state bar association referral program.

Settlements

Most cases end with a settlement, and yours probably will, too, although it may not come until the very last second. Settlements can be the best result because:

- Both parties feel like they won in some way.
- Neither spouse has to say unpleasant things about the other in court.
- Settlements cost less than lengthy trials.
- A settlement fits your needs and situation while decisions by judges are often less personal.

As you progress through your case, your attorney will probably be constantly working to reach some kind of settlement, and he or she will come to you from time to time with different proposals. Your attorney will advise you as to what is reasonable in your case, but you'll be the one who ultimately decides whether or not to accept a settlement. See Chapter 11 for more information about creating and working through settlements.

7

Gathering Household and Personal Documents

Documentation is an important part of the divorce process. Because so much of your divorce deals with financial and property matters, you need to put together and prepare to share paperwork that corresponds to your household and personal affairs. These documents are important because they show how much money you and your spouse have, the amount of debts you owe, what your monthly living expenses are (essential when determining child support), and what other property you own.

It can feel dehumanizing to realize that most of your divorce comes down to money and belongings, but remember that you need money and financial assets to help you live after the divorce. While it can be tempting to get fed up with the constant discussions about money and debts, you need to stay focused and try to provide as much documentation as you can in order to protect yourself. There is a direct payoff in monetary terms: the more proof you can provide, the better your chances of getting a financial settlement or decision that is in your favor.

Some couples are able to see a way to divide things fairly. Others fight tooth and nail over every last knickknack. In both situations, it's really important to provide your attorney with complete and accurate records. It's not uncommon to find that although you've agreed to split things in an equal way, your spouse is holding back some assets or information that you need to know about. The only way to protect yourself (and your children if you have them) is to be thorough.

How to Gather Documents

There are several steps involved in gathering the paperwork you need. Many items, such as bank statements, utility bills, social security numbers, and investment reports, are usually readily available in your household files. Other documents, such as life insurance, stocks, bonds, and even cash, are sometimes kept in a fireproof safe in the home or in a safe-deposit box, so be sure to check there.

You need to locate documents from the last twelve months if possible. If your spouse has made substantial withdrawals from accounts or investments within the last several years, you will want to provide documentation of this, particularly if the money was invested into his or her business or spent by him or her individually.

As you go through the Checklist of Documents to Gather at the end of this chapter, check off the documents you have located; then go back and tackle the ones you are missing. If you are missing current statements from banks, insurance companies, investments, or utility companies, call them and ask for copies. You may be able to access some accounts online.

Working with Your Spouse

Since both you and your spouse have attorneys, you're going to need two copies of each document. If one of you raids the files first, the other will have no access. Sure, this is a way to get back at your spouse, but your spouse's attorney will eventually obtain access to the missing documents, either through a process called discovery (when both sides in a case share requested information) or by subpoenaing the information from the company itself. Having your spouse's attorney chase these documents will cost money. Although the bill for that work will go to your spouse, it will come out of the pot of money you're dividing. Additionally, your attorney will generate billable hours responding to the request for the documents, which will come directly out of your pocket. It's more cost-effective to make copies of the documents and share them, as long as your attorney agrees the document contains information that needs to be shared. If you are trying to conceal assets or income from your spouse, discuss this with your attorney.

When You Can't Get Certain Documents

You may not be able to find or access certain documents. For example, if your spouse owns a business, he or she will probably be advised by his or her attorney to make sure you can't access financial information about the business. You also won't be able to access information from your spouse's employer or information about any individual accounts he or she holds. This is information your attorney will obtain for you. If you are able to get your hands on information about these things, make copies and don't take originals.

Organizing Documents

Once you have gathered the items on the checklist, you need to organize them. First make a copy of everything. Give one copy to your attorney and keep one for yourself as a backup. You will probably need to create separate envelopes or file folders for each of the subcategories listed in this chapter. Keep all the folders in the section of your accordion folder labeled "Household Documents." It is not a good idea to place original titles, birth certificates, or other important documents in your accordion folder. Keep the originals in a safe place at home or in your safe-deposit box, and place copies in your accordion folder.

65

Next you need to sort the documents. Put household expenses together. Place bank statements together. Gather credit card bills together. Put retirement and investment income together. Try to keep them in chronological order.

Since divorce is a lengthy process, you will constantly be obtaining new documents as bills and statements come each month. Make copies of them and place them in your accordion folder with the other relevant documents. This way you will always have current information in one place. Your attorney will not need copies of all of these documents. For example, he or she is not going to need a copy of your cable bill but will need copies of investments and bank accounts as well as outstanding debts. You need to keep all of these documents, though, because if they are ever challenged by your spouse, you need to be able to prove the amounts. It might seem overcautious to keep everything, but you only need to do this while your divorce is pending.

Analyzing Documents

Your attorney will analyze the documents you bring him or her to get a clear picture of what your property is worth. For example, the deed to your home gives your attorney basic information about ownership but offers no valuation of the home. A fair market rate has to be determined in order to create a property settlement. To reduce your attorney costs, you can do some of this legwork yourself.

- Get a market value for your home. Have a real estate agent come and pretend you are interested in selling. He or she will bring a printout of what similar homes have sold for in your area. This will narrow down the value of your home.
- Look up blue book values. Go to the library or online at www.kbb.com and find out the blue book values of any automobiles you and your spouse own. Locate guides for other items as well, such as boats, RVs, and motorcycles.
- Use pricing guides. If you and your spouse have valuable collections, use collector's guides to determine how much they are worth, or consider paying for an appraisal by an expert.

CHECKLIST OF DOCUMENTS TO GATHER

Personal

Personal documents are used to prove identity, social security number, address, and dates of birth and marriage.

☐ social security cards for you, your spouse, and your children (writing down the numbers is sufficient)

☐ marriage license

☐ life insurance policies

☐ birth certificates

Household

Household documents are used to prove living expenses and the cost of maintaining your household.

☐ mortgage statement or stub

☐ home equity loan statement

☐ home owner's or renter's insurance bill

☐ lease (if you are renting)

☐ car insurance bill

☐ electric bills

☐ gas bills

☐ water bills

☐ cable bills

☐ Internet access bills

☐ local and long-distance phone bills

☐ cell phone bills

☐ any outstanding home repair or contractor bills

Financial

Your attorney uses a wide range of documents to prove financial net worth.

☐ checking account statements

☐ savings account statements

☐ children's bank accounts

☐ other bank account statements

☐ credit union statements

☐ total of cash stored in the home and elsewhere

☐ investment statements

☐ copies of stocks and bonds

☐ retirement account statements (IRAs, Keough plans, 401(k)s, other)

☐ annuities

☐ 529 college saving plan statements

☐ trust paperwork

☐ tax returns for the last five years

☐ financial statements completed (such as loan applications)

Health Care

These documents will help your attorney establish your current health care insurance coverage, any contributions made to it, as well as outstanding medical bills that will need to be paid.

☐ health insurance card

☐ dental insurance card

☐ vision insurance card

☐ unpaid bills from health care providers

☐ pay stubs showing amounts you contribute for insurance

Debt

These documents will help your attorney establish your total current marital debt so that it can be divided.

- ☐ Visa statements
- ☐ MasterCard statements
- ☐ Discover Card statements
- ☐ American Express statements
- ☐ Diner's Club statements
- ☐ other credit card statements
- ☐ personal loan statements
- ☐ other loan statements
- ☐ evidence of family loans

Employment

Your attorney needs documentation to verify your income and benefits as well as your spouse's.

- ☐ your pay stubs for the last month
- ☐ your spouse's pay stubs for the last month
- ☐ commission or bonus stubs or statements in the last year
- ☐ reimbursed business expenses
- ☐ other benefits

Self-Owned Businesses

Documentation will help your attorney value the worth of businesses you or your spouse own.

- ☐ balance sheets
- ☐ accounts receivable
- ☐ accounts payable

- [ ] bank statements
- [ ] tax returns
- [ ] contracts
- [ ] offers to purchase the business
- [ ] profit-and-loss statements

Titles and Deeds
Deeds and titles will prove the existence and value of large assets such as real estate and vehicles.

- [ ] your car title
- [ ] your spouse's car title
- [ ] other vehicle titles
- [ ] boat or motorcycle title
- [ ] deed to the home and other real estate
- [ ] tax bill for real estate

Other
Don't overlook your less-obvious assets.

- [ ] frequent-flier miles
- [ ] season tickets
- [ ] time-shares
- [ ] medical savings accounts
- [ ] child care savings accounts
- [ ] stock options
- [ ] gym or club memberships
- [ ] patents, copyrights, royalties, license agreements

8

Documenting Your Income and Living Expenses

If you have children, you will be required to provide details about your monthly living expenses to help calculate child support. Your monthly expenses are also important if you are seeking alimony, or spousal support. In most states, you have to complete a financial affidavit that lists all of your income and expenses and shows a monthly living expense amount, whether or not alimony and child support are at issue.

While most of us have a general sense of how much we spend per month, we don't usually have a detailed monthly budget or list of expenditures. In order to provide the court with accurate information, you need to create a monthly budget for your living expenses. Most people find that this is actually an enlightening exercise; they learn a lot about their spending habits and are able to control their expenses. Creating a budget is also useful because after the divorce, you'll be responsible for all of these expenses yourself. Getting a sense of what they are now can help you plan for the post-divorce period.

How to Document Expenses

While it is usually acceptable to estimate some portions of your monthly expenses for the court's purposes, doing a true expense log is a very helpful exercise for you and your attorney because it gives you a realistic number to work with. At the end of this chapter you will find an Income Log and an Expense Log. Use them to record all of your income and expenses for one calendar month.

Include on the Expense Log all the items you actually pay for during the one-month period. Note that this log might not be an accurate reflection of your financial situation after the divorce. For example, if your spouse is currently making the mortgage payments on your home and you are living in it, you won't have anything recorded on your log for rent or mortgage. Or you might be paying the car insurance bill, which includes both your car and your spouse's. This is fine, as long as you make a note of all the things that are not reflected in your log, as well as the things that are listed but will change after the divorce, so that your attorney can understand.

When completing the Income Log, record only income that you bring into your household. This includes all of your reportable income for the month. It does not include garage sale or eBay income unless those kinds of sales are your business. You can choose to record pretax or after-tax income, but if you record pretax income, you will need to list taxes and other pay deductions on the Expense Log. You can store all of your pay stubs or income receipts in the "Monthly Expenses" pocket of your accordion file and then record them all at the end of the month. Make sure you transfer these to the "Household Documents" pocket once you have recorded all of the income for the month.

Using the Expense Log, record every expense you pay over the one-month period and add them up. This includes checks you write, bills you pay, and items you purchase in cash. Credit card expenses should be recorded when you pay the bill, not when the charges are incurred. You might want to keep a running tally in your wallet, purse, or PDA to track cash expenditures—you'll be surprised at how they add up.

If you and your spouse are still living together, you may need to estimate what your costs will be when you physically separate. If you are planning to move out, estimate what your expenses will be in an apartment. If your spouse is going to move out, determine if this will lower the monthly household costs.

Now comes the ugly part. Compare your total monthly income to your total monthly expenses. Don't panic if your expenses are higher than your income. This happens often, and it means that you overestimated something or that you are relying on your spouse's income. In practical terms, it's good for your case because it demonstrates that you don't have a lot of money to spend on alimony or child support or, conversely, that you need financial support.

Creating a Budget

Once you know how much you really are spending, use these numbers to create a budget. A budget is an estimated list of monthly expenses. While an expense log gives you a snapshot picture of what you are spending each month, a budget gives an average monthly total and includes the average amount of expenses that are paid on a yearly or quarterly basis. The budget is what you will use to complete divorce-related paperwork.

To create a budget, go through each item on the Monthly Budget worksheet at the end of this chapter and list an average monthly amount, realizing, for example, that gas or electricity costs go up at certain times of the year. If you have not separated, use your current joint living expenses. If you have separated, use your single expenses. Use average monthly costs for things that you pay less frequently than monthly, such as vacation expenses, holiday gifts, car registration fees, license renewal costs, club memberships, and so on. Come up with a yearly total for these and divide by twelve to find an average monthly figure.

Some items in the budget may not apply to you. For example, if your children will not be living with you full time, you may not be responsible for some of their expenses (at least until you start paying child support). Don't forget that this budget is supposed to be for you as a single person (or as a single head of household if you have kids), so don't include things such as your spouse's magazine subscriptions or his or her car expenses. If you are unsure who will be handling certain joint expenses such as credit cards, home equity loans, and other payments, leave them off, but be sure to mention them to your attorney. Use the Unresolved Joint Expenses form at the end of this chapter to document these items. Including them in your budget implies that you intend to take full responsibility for them after the divorce, and that's not an impression you want to give. Also include all expenses for everyone who will continue to live with you in the household. So, for example, where the form asks for tuition, you would include tuition for yourself as well as any children in your family.

Once you have completed the Monthly Budget worksheet, total it to obtain an average monthly living expense. Then take a few minutes to think about it. Are there places you can cut expenses? Think about what you can do to improve your financial picture once your divorce is over and you're on your own. Remember that if alimony or child support is an issue in your case, it is generally a good strategy to make it appear as if your monthly expenses are large. This doesn't mean you should artificially inflate them, but it is a good idea to err on the side of high estimates as opposed to low ones.

INCOME LOG

Make copies of this log for further use. List all actual income you bring into the household this month.

Income Log for the Month of _____

Date	Type/Description	Amount

Total _____

EXPENSE LOG ▶

Make copies of this log for further use. It should include all the expenses you actually pay for your household, including for children.

Expense Log for the Month of _____

Date	Type/Description	Amount

Total _____

MONTHLY BUDGET ▶

Household

Rent/mortgage _____
Home equity loan payments _____
Real estate taxes (if not included in mortgage) _____
Home owner's (if not included in mortgage) or
    renter's insurance _____
Home owner's association fees _____
Gas _____
Water _____
Electric _____
Telephone (local and long-distance calls) _____
Cell phone _____
Internet access and e-mail _____
Cable _____
Home repairs _____
Appliances and appliance maintenance _____
Food (include takeout but not dining out) _____
Alcohol _____
Household supplies _____
Children's school and activity expenses _____
Children's allowances _____
Pet food and supplies _____
Vet expenses _____
Household help _____
Charitable donations _____
Furniture purchases or maintenance _____
Lawn and yard expenses _____
Other _____

Personal

Clothing _____
Coin laundry and dry cleaning _____
Haircuts and styling _____

Gym membership _____

Personal care (nails, salon, facials, shoe shine) _____

Other club memberships _____

Life insurance premiums _____

Health insurance premiums _____

Health insurance copayments _____

Prescription costs _____

Vision care costs _____

Dental costs _____

Medical supplies or equipment _____

Hobbies _____

Tobacco expenses _____

Other _____

Financial

Monthly contributions to retirement accounts _____

Taxes _____

Bank charges _____

Finance charges on credit cards _____

Payments and finance charges on personal loans _____

Monthly contributions to medical savings accounts _____

Other monthly deductions from pay not included elsewhere _____

Transportation

Car loan or lease payment _____

Auto insurance _____

Repairs and maintenance _____

Average for license, inspection, and registration _____

Bus, taxi, train, plane costs _____

Gas _____

Car wash _____

Parking and tolls _____

Other vehicle expenses (include boat, motorcycle,
   RV, other cars) _____

Other _____

Entertainment
Dining out _____
Movies, theater, shows, attractions _____
Books, newspapers, magazines _____
Video/DVD rentals _____
Vacation _____
Babysitters _____
Other _____

Gifts
Holiday gifts (include all holidays you buy gifts for) _____
Birthday, anniversary, wedding, baby, hostess, retirement gifts _____
Cards, wrapping paper, gift bags, decorations _____
Other _____

School
Tuition _____
School books and supplies _____
Student loan payments _____
Activity and sports fees _____
Uniforms and equipment _____
Day care _____
After-school day care _____

Other
_____
_____
_____
_____
_____
_____
_____
_____
_____
_____
_____
_____
_____

UNRESOLVED JOINT EXPENSES

Description	Amount

9

Large Assets

Dividing large or important assets in a fair way can be difficult because they may not be things you can easily cut in half, or because the value of the asset might be greater than the total of all your other assets. Contested divorces often include division of pensions, investments, vehicles, homes, and second homes, as well as the value of businesses, professional licenses, and degrees. Future potential earnings aren't divided as assets, but they are part of the consideration for alimony.

Because your large assets are worth so much, you want to gather as much information about them as you can to maximize your settlement or award. Accurate valuations are also important so these items can be divided fairly.

Separate Versus Marital Property

The first step in property division is determining which large assets are separate property and which are marital. Things that were acquired during the marriage—even if they are owned in one name only—are marital property and must be considered in your property division. Separate property, sometimes called premarital property, cannot be divided in a divorce. It includes things owned before marriage, received through gift or inheritance during marriage, or awarded as a personal injury settlement during marriage.

There's one point you need to know about separate property: a portion of an item that is separate property can be considered marital property if the nonowner spouse contributed to its upkeep or increased its value during marriage. Assume, for example, that you owned a home before you were married and rented it out to tenants while you were married. If your spouse painted, mowed the lawn, or fixed the plumbing while you were married, he or she contributed to the upkeep of that property and would be entitled to receive a portion of the increase in its value that occurred because of his or her input. Similarly, if your spouse owned a business prior to marriage and you helped out at the business during your marriage (and did not receive a salary), you would be entitled to a portion of the increase in value that occurred during that time.

If you are the nonowner spouse, use the Contribution to Separate Asset worksheet at the end of this chapter to document your involvement with the asset. Write down all the ways you've assisted with or contributed to an asset that your spouse owns separately.

Use the Large Asset Separate Property Log at the end of this chapter to document items you own separately.

Understanding Nonconcrete Assets

Everything acquired during a marriage is considered marital property and is subject to division. This includes intangibles such as degrees, professional licenses, businesses, retirement accounts, and even frequent-flier miles.

A degree or professional license that was earned while you were married, such as a medical degree or a license to style hair, is considered marital property even though it is not technically "divided" in a divorce settlement. The court can't give you your spouse's M.B.A., but its value can be included in the total pot of assets, and you will probably be entitled to some cash value if you provided support while the license or degree was being earned. Even if your spouse is not currently using the degree (he or she is still in school, for example, or is staying home with the children), it is still an item of property that has a value. After all, should he or she put the degree to use sometime in the future, it will enhance his or her earning power.

How Large Assets Are Divided

When a property settlement or division is made in your case, you won't each get half of every asset. It would be difficult—and often impossible—to give each spouse one-half of a car, a house, a business, or a degree. Instead, all of the assets will be valued and totaled, and you will each receive half of the total value or whatever amount a court decides is equitable. One of you might get the house, for example, while the other might get the investments. Large assets are often balanced with debt. The spouse who gets the house might also be solely responsible for the mortgage.

Finding Large Assets

To ensure that your property division is going to be fair (and that you will get as much as possible), you need to create a complete list of large marital assets. Use the List of Large Joint Assets at the end of this chapter for that purpose.

Get together all account statements. If you need information on your or your spouse's retirement account or pension plan, call the plan administrator and request a current statement. Think carefully about intangible assets such as licenses, degrees, and businesses—they may have value. Also include items that you might not consider important. For example, if your spouse has a motorcycle or a collection of Depression glass, you should list these items even if you have no interest in them, because they increase the total pot of assets.

If you list professional licenses or degrees, indicate what they are and the dates they were awarded. For a degree, indicate the years it took to earn it.

Finding Hidden Assets

You might think it is difficult to hide high-value assets, but many spouses have done so. It is particularly easy to do if one spouse has a business. Joint assets or funds can be funneled into the business to hide them from the other spouse. You should also be suspicious if your spouse has recently taken a trip to a foreign country where it may be possible to conceal cash in secret bank accounts. In most cases, though, you'll probably sense if your spouse is trying to hide something and where it is hidden. If you do believe your spouse is hiding a large amount of money, talk to your attorney about the possibility of hiring a private investigator to track it down.

Make copies of all account statements you can find, especially those that are in your spouse's name alone. Make note of large cash withdrawals from joint or sole accounts. Cash is hard to trace, but if you can prove that your spouse has withdrawn it, you have a convincing piece of evidence.

Types of Large Assets

There are different types of large assets, and you will need to obtain different information for each of them.

Accounts

Assets such as investments, bank accounts, and CDs can be easy to value. All you need is an account statement. Other items can be harder to value.

Retirement Accounts

You have two choices for how to divide pensions and retirement accounts. You can determine a current cash value (what the account is worth today), for which you will need an accountant, and give the nontitled spouse a portion of that value. Or you can agree that the nontitled spouse will receive a certain percentage of the payments when they are made.

If you are the owner, you might prefer to settle up now so you won't have to worry about it later, but it sometimes makes more sense to choose the long-term approach. If you or your spouse should die before retirement, no payments will be made.

If you are the nonowner spouse, a bird in hand might be better than two in the bush in this case. If you take a cash settlement now, you can invest it or do what you like with it. If you choose to wait, you or your spouse might die before retirement, leaving you with nothing. As always, this is a choice you should discuss with your attorney before making any decisions.

Businesses

You need a specialized accountant to value a business, and it can be an expensive and time-consuming effort, so consider how large or small the business is before you decide to go that route. It is usually a bad idea for two former spouses to continue to co-own a company. Talk to your attorney about this. A cash settlement or buyout may make more sense, but it depends on your particular situation.

Real Estate

Real estate can generally be appraised by local real estate agents or real estate appraisers. You can also go to your county clerk's office and look up homes comparable to yours that sold recently to find out what the sale price was (you will need to know the addresses to obtain this information). Do not rely on your property tax assessment. While it can be a good starting point, it is often wildly different from the price you can get for a home on the market. Remember that when you value a home, you have to find out what it would sell for and then subtract the mortgage owed to determine how much value you own.

Licenses and Degrees

You need a specialized accountant to value licenses and degrees. Sometimes these items are valued as part of a business or practice (such as a medical practice) and sometimes they are valued by themselves. Since this is a complicated area of law that varies from state to state and uses different formulas and rules, it is important to talk to your attorney about how these items are valued in your state.

Once you have obtained information about the value of your large assets, store the documents in the "Large Assets" pocket of your accordion file.

CONTRIBUTION TO SEPARATE ASSET

Use this worksheet to describe your contributions to your spouse's separately owned assets during the marriage. Make copies for each asset.

Asset _____

Contributions

_____

_____

_____

_____

_____

_____

_____

_____

_____

_____

_____

_____

_____

_____

_____

_____

_____

_____

_____

_____

_____

LARGE ASSET SEPARATE PROPERTY LOG

List large assets that are your separate property. Make copies of this log for further use.

Description	When and How Acquired

LIST OF LARGE JOINT ASSETS

Make copies of this log for further use.

Description	Account Number (if any)	Location	Approximate Value

10 ▶

Documenting Debts

The good news is that even though you have to divide assets in a divorce, you also get to divide your debts. Debts can be divided equally or based on considerations of fairness. For example, the spouse with the higher income might be held responsible for more of the debt, or the spouse keeping the car might take on the car loan.

Separate and Marital Debts

Debts, like assets, can be separate or marital. Debts you incurred prior to marriage will be your separate responsibility, and the same goes for your spouse, even if you worked together to pay down the premarital debts. Remember that even if a debt is listed in one name only, it is considered a joint or marital debt if it was taken out during the marriage.

Use the List of Spouse's Separate Debts worksheet at the end of this chapter to create a list of your spouse's separate debts so that you do not become responsible for paying them.

Organizing Your Debt

There are two kinds of debt to consider: recurring and long-term.

Recurring debts—rent and utility bills, for example—are those that happen on a regular basis, are paid, and then occur again. Hopefully, you and your spouse are in a position to pay these bills as they arise. Recurring debts don't need to be divided, because as soon as you separate, or as soon as your divorce concludes, you will each have your own set of recurring debts and you will pay them on your own. However, if you have arrears, balances, and penalties, these need to be included in your list of debts.

Long-term debts are the ones to be concerned about when facing divorce. You need to create a complete list of these debts with current balances due. Use the List of Joint Debts at the end of the chapter to organize that information. Place copies of all loan statements and other debt-related documents in the appropriate pocket of your accordion file. Even if you have included these items elsewhere, it is a good idea to keep copies of them here so you have all debt information in one place.

When listing debts, be sure to include:

- car loans and leases
- mortgages
- home equity loans
- personal loans (unsecured loans)
- student loans
- lines of credit (such as overdraft)
- loans against life insurance
- loans against retirement or pension accounts
- loans from relatives or friends
- credit card balances (those not paid off each month)
- unpaid balances on utilities
- unpaid health care bills
- installment payments
- late rent

Do not include business loans. These will be deducted against the value of the business.

If you are unsure of what you owe on a specific loan, call the creditor. If you think you have other debts outstanding but can't put your finger on what they are, look through your checkbook to see who you make payments to on a regular basis. If you still can't find the information, order your credit report. See Chapter 2 to find out how to order a credit report.

LIST OF SPOUSE'S SEPARATE DEBTS

Make copies of this log for further use.

Creditor	Account Number	Current Balance

LIST OF JOINT DEBTS

Make copies of this log for further use.

Creditor	Account Number	Current Balance

◄11►

Reaching Settlements and Dividing Household Belongings

Yꜱou will find that there are many things you and your spouse can decide on your own. Some of these agreements will be informal, small decisions, such as who will take the dishes, while others will be large decisions, such as how you will arrange custody or divide debt. This chapter will help you work out small household issues as well as larger settlements.

Negotiating Settlements

As you work through your case, use the Settlement List at the end of this chapter to organize your household belongings into three categories—must have, unsure, and don't want. Do this for possessions as well as custody, visitation, child support, and alimony. Make sure you create a payment range for child support and alimony with the lowest and highest amounts you want to receive or pay out.

During negotiations, your attorney will probably advise you to pretend that you want some of the things on your don't-want list and that you must have some of the things on your unsure list. This strategy will allow you to bargain for things you truly must have. Never reveal your range for alimony or child support to your spouse. If you are negotiating on your own, pick a number that is less than you are willing to pay or more than you need to receive. This will give you room to negotiate.

As you move through the divorce, you'll probably change your mind a few times about where certain items belong on your list, so be prepared to rewrite it as you go. Mark in the unsure column items that you'd be willing to trade for other things you would rather have. This will help identify items to offer in a settlement.

You will need to consider all elements of your divorce in the settlement process—custody, child support, alimony, property division, and debt resolution. Settlements are complicated processes that involve careful calculations of retirement benefits, appraisal value, and income potential as well as custody and visitation issues. You aren't always trading apples for apples, meaning that you might, for example, agree to accept a larger property settlement in exchange for less alimony. Listen to your attorney's advice about settlements.

Your proposal has to be reasonable or it is unlikely that your spouse, let alone a judge, will agree to it. Unless your attorney recommends it, don't waste everyone's time proposing a settlement that gives you everything and your spouse nothing. Use these guidelines to evaluate settlement offers:

- Do you feel comfortable with the terms of the settlement?
- Are you getting everything that is really important to you?
- Does the settlement allow you to manage financially?
- Does the settlement give you most of your "must haves"?
- Have all assets and debts been taken into account?
- Have you had enough time to really consider the settlement?
- Are the compromises things you can live with?
- Does the settlement make you feel cheated?
- Do you feel pressured into settling by your attorney or your spouse?

Any agreement you make with your spouse on your own is an informal settlement, meaning that it is unenforceable if one of you goes back on your word. For this reason, it is important to consult your attorney about large settlement issues and to have everything formalized. Your attorney can present a settlement to the court, and the judge will incorporate it into the final divorce order. Your attorney can also draw up settlement papers that you and your spouse can sign to make an agreement official.

Dividing Household Items

Furniture, dishes, electronics, photo albums, jewelry, and special collections carry a lot of meaning and are important items for daily living. Dividing these items can be difficult because many of them were purchased jointly during the marriage. In addition, it can be quite a task to sort through everything you've accumulated while married.

Separate Property

Before tackling the long list of household items that you will divide, you need to make a list of items that are separate property. Separate property includes items that each of you owned before marrying as well as items either of you received as gifts (even from each other) or inheritances during the marriage. List these on the Separate Property Items form at the end of this chapter. These things are yours, and your spouse has no claim to them.

Marital Property

Items acquired during the marriage are referred to as marital property (or community property in some states). These items belong to both of you, and during the divorce you or the court will have to determine who gets them.

For many people, division of marital property becomes symbolic of the divorce. They want to "win" and come out with the most stuff. They take things to punish their spouse, or they rely on belongings to represent their self-worth. Try to think rationally about your possessions. Letting your spouse take the DVD player doesn't mean he or she has "won." It doesn't symbolize anything if you don't let it. Don't view the property settlement as a way to hurt your spouse; it's not worth $150 an hour to have your attorney negotiate the division of minor things. Focus on the items you will get the most use out of or that you need the most.

The best plan is to figure out the division of household items with your spouse, if possible. Many items will be easy to divide. You may have no interest in the big screen TV, the sewing kit, the ceramic figurines, the ironing board, or the power tools. Duplicates are also easy to divide—one to each of you.

Follow these suggestions when dividing things:

95

- Try not to break up sets (such as a matching couch and loveseat or a set of china). Sets have more value when they are together.
- Take items you want or will use. Don't take things out of spite or revenge.
- Try to keep most of the children's belongings or items they use the most in the household in which the children will live.
- Make sure the household the children will live in is comfortable and safe.
- Recognize that you each will have to purchase replacements for some household items. No one is going to walk away from this with everything.
- Focus first on dividing items according to obvious needs; worry later about making things fair.
- Focus on use, not on value. Bottom-line value can be adjusted later.
- Your lifestyle is going to be different after your divorce, so focus on what you will need in your new life and leave behind things that are part of your old life.

As you sort through things, try to be sensitive to what your spouse wants to keep. Though you might think that a football jersey or a ceramic bear is worthless, he or she might want it. Throw out only those items you know no one wants. Donate items that are in good condition to a charity (such as Goodwill or the Salvation Army) and get a receipt to use as a tax deduction. You might also consider holding a garage sale or selling things on eBay and splitting the proceeds.

The division of household items usually begins before the divorce does, and it occurs not in an afternoon, but over a period of months. One spouse moves out and takes some things. Over the following weeks, he or she comes back for more items, a few at a time. If you are concerned about bottom-line value equality, document this ongoing property division. You will want this information when you divide items formally.

Problems can also arise when one spouse takes items without telling the other. If this happens to you, it is a long, hard road to get these items back. List everything you think is missing on the form titled Items Taken Without Agreement and give the list to your attorney. Your attorney will work to get some items returned by agreement or will include these items in the things you are asking the court to award to you. Otherwise, these items will be included in the total net worth of all assets so that you will at least receive half of their value.

Once you have divided the undisputed items, fill out the Agreed-Upon Items to Divide list at the end of this chapter to specify who is getting what. It's a good idea for both of you to initial or sign the list to indicate your agreement. This will be useful in resolving future disputes and will help you create a fair overall division of items.

Appraising Items

Although you probably know what each item cost when you bought it or what it would sell for new today, in a divorce you need to come up with a value that reflects an item's condition and age. The couch that you paid $1,000 for when it was new may be worth only $200 if you were to resell it now. If you don't know what something is worth, look in the classifieds or on eBay.

Although as a practical matter you'll probably be splitting up most of your marital property, things that can be classified as sets or collections have a greater value together than they would if valued singly and added together. Following are some items that can be valued as groups:

- CDs
- books
- tapes
- videos
- DVDs
- houseplants
- silverware
- dishes
- pots and pans
- tools
- items in a collection
- decorations
- software
- linens and towels
- lawn tools
- sets of furniture
- glassware

When it comes to negotiating, you always want to value the items your spouse is taking at a higher value than the items you are taking.

Disputed Items

Now that you've split up the uncontested items, it's time to get down to the nitty-gritty of negotiating the rest. Begin by filling out the Disputed Items to

Divide list at the end of this chapter. Some couples are able to make this list together, while others find they need to do it alone to avoid arguments. Do whatever works for you. In either case, you'll probably need to negotiate the value of the items.

When you have compiled your list, make a copy of it. Then sit down by yourself with the list and put a check in front of each item you definitely want. Put a question mark in front of items you would like but are willing to give up in exchange for other items.

Once you know what you want, go through the list with your spouse, using the unmarked copy, and indicate items you would like. Include the items you checked on your copy as well as some that were question marks. Act as if you really want the questionable items initially and then give them up as a compromise. If you use this tactic, though, keep in mind that your spouse knows you well and may be able to tell when you are bluffing.

Try to be reasonable during negotiations. Remember, these are only material possessions. It may be helpful to set some ground rules before you begin. Agree that you will:

- not raise your voices or insult each other
- treat it as a business meeting
- meet without the children present
- meet in a neutral or private place
- try not to discuss other issues involved with the divorce at that time

When dividing disputed items, consider pairing up items of similar value. Suggestions like "you take the freezer and I'll take the fridge," or "you take one dresser and I'll take the other" can really jump-start the process. If you are unable to agree upon certain items, talk to your attorney or mediator about how to divide them.

Total the value of the items you've each taken on the Disputed Items to Divide list and add the total from the list of items you had no dispute over or that were previously divided. Compare your totals. They don't have to be equal. In most states, marital property is divided in a way that is fair but not necessarily equal (sometimes called equitable distribution). The important thing is that you both feel the property division is fair. If you want to have a completely equal division, you will need to factor in large items, investments, real estate, and cash.

98

SETTLEMENT LIST

Make copies of this log for further use.

Must Have	Unsure	Don't Want

SEPARATE PROPERTY ITEMS

List items owned prior to the marriage. Make copies of this log for
further use.

_____

_____

_____

_____

_____

_____

_____

_____

_____

_____

_____

_____

_____

_____

_____

_____

_____

_____

_____

_____

_____

_____

_____

ITEMS TAKEN WITHOUT AGREEMENT

Description	Value	Date Taken

AGREED-UPON ITEMS TO DIVIDE

Make copies of this log for further use.

Item	Approximate Value	Owner

Total value of wife's items _____

Total value of husband's items _____

DISPUTED ITEMS TO DIVIDE ▶

Make copies of this log for further use.

Item	Value	Owner

Total value of wife's items _____

Total value of husband's items _____

12

Child Support

Child support is calculated on the basis of parental income, which is determined in most states by completing a detailed form. Once income is determined, a percentage is applied to child support based on the number of children. Child support has to do with children from this marriage only. Children from another marriage or relationship do not play a part in the calculation unless they have been adopted by the other spouse. Talk with your attorney about the laws in your state, and ask how child support will be figured.

Purpose of Child Support

Child support is not meant to be a punishment for the parent paying it or a free ride for the parent receiving it. It is intended to ensure that children can maintain the same lifestyle after a divorce that they had before. Although child support is based on the parents' incomes, it is meant to benefit the child. Even so, the parent who receives it is not required to document that the money was spent to support the children.

Temporary Child Support

A temporary order of child support is often made during a case so that the parent who is living with the child most of the time will have ongoing support. The amount is temporary until a final order of child support is handed down at the end of the case.

Calculating Child Support

If you are the parent who will be paying child support, it's important to understand that the amount is going to be calculated primarily on your income. As you work with your attorney, your general strategy will be to minimize your income whenever possible. The more income you show, the more you will end up paying. You must report your income honestly to the court, but your attorney can help you find ways to minimize the amount you report. You need to talk with your attorney if your spouse has knowledge of any income you don't report to the IRS.

Another part of your general strategy is to help the court see all of your spouse's income. Your attorney might want to imply that your spouse has a higher income or a greater earning potential than he or she is disclosing. This may seem a little underhanded, but keep in mind that the whole point is to make it appear as if your spouse does not need the amount of child support that is being requested. Tell your attorney if you're uncomfortable with this tactic.

If you are the parent who will be receiving child support, you want to minimize your income and appear at a lower standard of living than your spouse. Your strategy will be to gather as much information as you can about your spouse's earnings. If you have information about unreported income, share this with your attorney. Although some people feel satisfaction in alerting the IRS to a spouse's unreported income, both spouses who sign the tax return are generally liable to the IRS for these omissions. Because they can backfire, it's best to hold off on vengeful tactics like this until you can discuss the implications with your attorney.

Other Child Support Amounts

A court can raise a child support award above the base amount in response to factors such as the incomes of the parents, the lifestyle to which the child is accustomed, and the child's special needs. In many states, medical care, school tuition, uniforms, lessons, sports equipment, extracurricular expenses, and more are added onto the base child support amount. The more expenses you can document, the more child support you will receive. Use the Children's Expenses form at the end of this chapter to record that information. Place corresponding receipts in the accordion folder pocket labeled "Children's Expenses." If you are the parent who will be paying child support, you want to minimize the expenses presented by your spouse as much as possible, keeping in mind that the goal is to make sure your children are supported adequately.

Most states require one parent to be responsible for providing health insurance for the child—normally whoever has family coverage available through an employer. The noncustodial parent—the one who pays child support—might have to pay health care expenses not covered by insurance as well. The court might also order the noncustodial parent to take out a life insurance policy on him- or herself with the children as beneficiaries. This is intended to provide ongoing financial support for the children if that parent dies and child support ends.

If you are the parent receiving child support and the other parent is required to pay uninsured health care expenses, you need to keep careful records of the children's uninsured medical expenses. The best method is to inform the provider that the other parent bears the financial responsibility and that he or she is to be billed directly for any uninsured expenses. However, unexpected health care problems do arise, and many providers require copayments to be made at the time of service. Pharmacies also require payment upon pickup. In these instances you may have to pay the expense out of pocket and seek repayment from the other parent. Use the Children's Uninsured Health Expenses form to record expenses and repayment. Give your spouse copies of the form and the receipts each month. Store originals in the accordion pocket labeled "Children's Uninsured Health Care Receipts" until they have been paid.

How Child Support Is Paid

Child support can be paid directly by one parent to the other, or it can be paid to a state child support collection agency, which then pays the custodial parent. Payments to the state can be made via automatic paycheck deduction.

Some judges will automatically order payments to be made through the state, while others may let the parties decide. Generally, if you are the person receiving child support, it is to your benefit to have it go through the state. The state will keep track of the payments and will contact the other parent if payments are missing. You won't have to discuss child support with your spouse because he or she will deal with the state. These agencies usually review and adjust the payment amounts on a regular basis to keep pace with inflation.

If you are the person paying child support, you may not want to have payments taken out of your paycheck. Also, if you make payments directly to the other parent, he or she will probably be forgiving if you are a day or two late in your payments once in a while, whereas the state will automatically record the delinquency and charge interest.

Tracking Child Support Payments

Whether you are paying or receiving child support, you need to document the payments. Even state agencies can make mistakes.

If you are paying child support, make sure you record every payment made. Missed payments and payments you made but can't prove if your spouse challenges them can result in a judgment against you and suspension of your driver's license. If you are making payments directly to the custodial parent, you may wish to ask him or her to sign a receipt acknowledging each payment. Copy the sample receipt at the end of this chapter and obtain one for each payment. Store the signed receipts in the accordion folder pocket labeled "Child Support Receipts." This is much simpler than having to obtain canceled checks from your bank. If you are making payments to a child support collection unit, record each payment on the Child Support Payment Log in this chapter.

The custodial parent can also use the Child Support Payment Log to track not only payments that were received, but also ones that were missed. The log will come in handy if the noncustodial parent claims to have made a payment in cash that was never received. If you are the custodial parent, never sign a receipt for payment without first receiving the payment.

Due Dates

When you first start to pay or receive child support, it's a good idea to include payment due dates on your master calendar. You probably won't need to do this after a few months, but in the beginning it is helpful to write it down so you don't miss a payment or so you can recognize when your spouse is late with a payment.

Nonpayment

Failure to pay child support can result in a judgment against the payer, revocation of driver's and other licenses, and even jail time.

Adjusting Child Support

As time goes by and your situation changes, you may need to adjust the amount of child support. If you are the payer and you lose your job, you might need to ask for a reduction. Or, if you are the payee and you know the other parent has received a pay raise, you might want to ask for more. To make these adjustments, you'll need to contact your attorney and return to court. You'll also need to document your reasons for requesting a change. If child support is being paid through your state child support collection agency, the agency may automatically adjust the amount every few years for inflation.

CHILDREN'S EXPENSES

List monthly amounts. For expenses that are less frequent than once a month, determine the yearly amount and then divide by 12 to reach the monthly cost.

Day care _____

Tuition _____

School or day care registration fees _____

Babysitting/nanny _____

After-school day care _____

School books _____

School supplies _____

School photos _____

Field trip expenses _____

Donations requested by the school _____

School event fees _____

Music/vocal lessons _____

Musical instrument rental or payment _____

Music supplies _____

Music competition fees _____

Band/orchestra/chorus uniforms or costumes _____

Music group photos _____

Sports uniforms _____

Sports supplies and equipment _____

Sports fees _____

Sports photos _____

Dance lessons _____

Dance supplies _____

Dance costumes _____

Dance competition fees _____

Dance photos _____

Girl or Boy Scout fees _____

Scout uniforms _____

Scout supplies _____

Scout photos _____

Extracurricular club membership fees _____

Extracurricular club supplies _____

Extracurricular photos _____

Other lesson or club fees _____

Other lesson or club supplies _____

Other group photos _____

Camp fees _____

Camp supplies _____

Tutoring _____

Approximate mileage per month for children's transportation _____

Children's transportation fees _____

Monthly children's clothing/footwear costs _____

Monthly children's hobby costs _____

Children's pets' costs _____

Birthday/holiday gifts _____

Gifts for children to take to birthday parties _____

Children's Internet access _____

Children's computer costs _____

Children's computer supplies _____

Children's telephone costs _____

Children's cell phone costs _____

School lunches _____

Entertainment _____

Toys and books _____

Regular medical/dental/orthodontic/vision/mental health
  supplies and services _____

Backpacks, bags, lunch boxes, purses _____

Allowance _____

Onetime expenses such as yearbooks, school rings,
  field trips, teacher gifts, school donations, school T-shirts,
  school photos (divide by 12) _____

                                        Total _____

CHILDREN'S UNINSURED HEALTH EXPENSES ▶

Copy this form and use one for each month of the year.

**Children's Uninsured Health Expenses
for the Month of** _____

Child	Date	Description	Cost	Date Payment Received

CHILD SUPPORT RECEIPTS

Make several copies of this page so that you can prepare a receipt for each month.

Child Support Receipt

I received $_____ from _____ on _____ (date)

for the period of _____ to _____ as child support.

_____
(signature)

Child Support Receipt

I received $_____ from _____ on _____ (date)

for the period of _____ to _____ as child support.

_____
(signature)

Child Support Receipt

I received $_____ from _____ on _____ (date)

for the period of _____ to _____ as child support.

_____
(signature)

Child Support Receipt

I received $_____ from _____ on _____ (date)

for the period of _____ to _____ as child support.

_____
(signature)

CHILD SUPPORT PAYMENT LOG

Make copies of this log for further use.

Date	Check Number	Amount	Payment Period	Check if Unpaid

Alimony

Alimony, or spousal support, is often awarded to help one spouse become self-supporting. It can also be used as a kind of property settlement; instead of a specified amount of cash or property, a spouse receives regular payments for a certain period of time. Alimony is rarely used as a way to punish a spouse for things he or she did that led to the end of the marriage.

Some people mistakenly think that one spouse automatically gets alimony in every divorce case. In fact, it's not the norm. For example, in some areas alimony is awarded only if a spouse needs assistance while going back to school or looking for a job. Talk to your attorney about the alimony laws in your state and find out when and how it is normally awarded.

How Alimony Is Awarded

When deciding if there will be alimony and how much will be awarded, judges usually consider these factors:

- **Length of the marriage.** Usually, the longer the marriage, the longer the payment period.
- **Health of the spouses.** If one spouse has a disability or an illness, he or she will more likely need financial support.
- **Parties' incomes and property.**

- **Parties' earning abilities and skills.** This would be a factor if one spouse stayed home with the children and had no income but had a medical degree and thus the potential to earn a decent living if he or she went back to work.
- **Lost earnings.** One spouse might have lost years of earnings because he or she stayed home to care for children.
- **Contributions each spouse made to the marriage financially and emotionally.** These would include nurturing children or supporting a spouse who earns a degree or starts a business.
- **Which parent the children live with.** This impacts the custodial parent's financial situation and needs.
- **Whether either spouse has wasted marital assets.**
- **How the parties treated the marital assets during the divorce.** If one spouse destroyed property or exhibited a careless attitude about conserving property, it would be considered.
- **Bad behavior by either party.** This would include emotional or physical abuse.

In many states, the rule of thumb is that alimony is granted for one-third of the length of the marriage; so a nine-year marriage would have a three-year alimony payment. Lifetime alimony can be awarded when a spouse is ill, elderly, or disabled, or it can be awarded as a onetime payment. The lump-sum payout is similar to a property settlement, but the tax consequences are different. One spouse can be ordered to pay the other's household expenses as a type of alimony.

116

Seeking Alimony

If you are seeking alimony, you want to minimize your own income, maximize your spouse's income, highlight the many unselfish contributions you made to the marriage, and show how your contributions limited your ability to earn an income. You also want to show that your spouse has depleted marital assets. Overall, you want to portray yourself as responsible and needy and your spouse as selfish, rich, and irresponsible.

You can receive temporary spousal support during the divorce as well as alimony after the case is decided.

Alimony Rules and Regulations

Any alimony or spousal support money you receive is taxable income and must be reported. Because alimony has tax consequences, and because the spouse paying alimony can be subject to contempt of court orders for failing to meet his or her obligation, it is imperative to keep careful records of alimony paid or received.

Talk with your attorney about balancing alimony with child support. If you are the spouse paying alimony and child support, it is more advantageous to pay a higher amount in alimony, because it is tax deductible and often ends sooner than child support obligations. If you are the spouse receiving alimony and child support, it is more advantageous to receive a higher child support payment, because you don't have to report it as income and it will probably have a longer duration than alimony. Alimony ends upon the death of either spouse and usually ends if the spouse receiving it remarries.

If you are seeking alimony, consult the list of considerations at the beginning of this chapter to build your case, and complete the Alimony Worksheet at the end of the chapter.

Tracking Alimony

If you are the spouse paying alimony, get a receipt. A cashed check is sufficient if you write "alimony" and the period it covers in the memo section. But since many banks no longer return checks without specific requests, it may be simpler to have your spouse sign a receipt for each payment. It is a good idea to pay by check whenever possible so that you have two kinds of proof of payment—the canceled check and the signed receipt. Receipts are necessary if you want to deduct alimony payments from your taxes or if you have to prove to a court that you made your payment. Use the Alimony Receipts at the end of the chapter and store them in the "Alimony Receipts" pocket in your accordion folder.

If you are the spouse receiving alimony, you need to track payments so that you have proof of a missed payment and accurate records to use when reporting alimony on your income taxes. Use the Alimony Payment Log to record this information.

Medical Insurance

If you were covered by your spouse's medical insurance policy during marriage, you are eligible to continue your coverage on the policy through a federal law called COBRA. COBRA allows you to continue your coverage for up to eighteen months, but you have to pay for it yourself unless the court orders your spouse to pay it as a form of alimony or property settlement. After eighteen months you will need to obtain your own policy.

ALIMONY WORKSHEET

Length of your marriage _____

Describe your health.

_____

_____

_____

_____

Describe differences in your and your spouse's income and property ownership.

_____

_____

_____

_____

Describe your earning ability and skills. What kind of education or training do you need to improve these? How long will it take to do so, and how much will it cost?

_____

_____

_____

_____

Describe anything you did that decreased your earning potential (such as staying home with the children). For how long did you do this? What position did you leave to do so? What did it pay?

_____

_____

_____

_____

Describe the contributions you made to the marriage, both financially and emotionally (time and energy you devoted to caring for the children, advancing your spouse's career, and so on).

_____

_____

_____

_____

With whom will the children be living after the marriage? _____

Has your spouse wasted or used up marital assets? Explain how he or she did so, and provide a value and description of the assets.

_____

_____

_____

_____

Describe anything your spouse did during the marriage that decreased the value of some marital assets.

_____

_____

_____

_____

Describe your spouse's abuse or unpleasantness toward you.

_____

_____

_____

_____

ALIMONY RECEIPTS

Make several copies of this page so that you can create receipts for future alimony payments that you make.

Alimony Receipt

I received $_____ from _____ on _____ (date)

for the period of _____ to _____ as alimony.

_____
(signature)

Alimony Receipt

I received $_____ from _____ on _____ (date)

for the period of _____ to _____ as alimony.

_____
(signature)

Alimony Receipt

I received $_____ from _____ on _____ (date)

for the period of _____ to _____ as alimony.

_____
(signature)

Alimony Receipt

I received $_____ from _____ on _____ (date)

for the period of _____ to _____ as alimony.

_____
(signature)

ALIMONY PAYMENT LOG ▶

Make copies of this log to track alimony that you receive.

Date	Check Number	Amount	Payment Period	Check if Unpaid

◀14▶

Custody and Visitation

If your divorce involves a dispute over custody and visitation (sometimes called "access" or "parenting time"), you're probably very concerned about how the court will decide. In most cases, the court will issue a temporary order of custody, deciding where the children will live and how they will split their time with the parents while the case is ongoing. Usually the court seeks to preserve the status quo, meaning that most of the time the children will remain where they are, and whatever arrangement you and your spouse have worked out will remain in place. If temporary custody and visitation are hotly disputed, you will have a hearing (a short trial) where your attorneys will provide evidence and the judge will make a decision.

While your case is ongoing, it is essential that you keep good records of how your children divide their time, as well as problems and concerns that arise about parenting.

Custody decisions are based upon what is in the best interest of the children—what overall parenting arrangement will work best for them and allow them to have normal and happy lives. Courts believe that it is important for children to have both parents in their lives whenever possible. The judge will look for a solution that will let your child spend time with both of you, in a way that makes the most sense for everyone involved.

The time during which your divorce is pending is the most crucial point for custody cases. During this time, everything you and your spouse do is under the watchful eye of the court. The way you parented before the divorce is important, but it isn't as obvious and immediate to the court. The way you and your spouse spend time with your children during the divorce will be what the court considers most heavily, simply because there will be the most evidence available about it.

Because of this, it is important that you create a record that reflects your point of view. If you are the parent who has temporary residential custody of the children, be sure to record all the time you spend with them as well as the times your spouse misses visitation. If you are the parent with temporary visitation, you want to create a record that shows you maximizing your time with your child and documents anything your spouse does to interfere with that.

Tips for Avoiding a Custody Trial

Custody trials can be painful, particularly for the children. Consider these ways to avoid a custody trial.

- Think long and hard about what kind of arrangement would work best for your child.
- Think about what kind of arrangement feels natural to you.
- Remember that your child has two parents and must have time with both.
- Keep in mind that there is a big difference between being a good spouse and being a good parent. You may not think much of your spouse as a partner, but that doesn't mean he or she isn't a good parent.
- Try not to get caught up in the words that designate how the time is divided—"custody" and "visitation" sound nasty. Focus instead on sharing time.
- Don't ask your child to make a decision or indicate a preference.
- Take an honest look at each parent's schedule and lifestyle and think about how the children fit into that schedule.
- Make it clear to the other parent that you want him or her to be an important part of the child's life.
- Try to talk with your spouse about what kind of arrangement will work best for the children.

- Think about parenting time as something that belongs to your children, not to you and your spouse.
- Think not in terms of who gets the most time, but in terms of what time-sharing arrangement will work best for your children, with emphasis on not disrupting the children's lifestyle.

Thinking About Custody and Visitation

The first impulse in a divorce is often to grab what you can and run, even with respect to the children. You want to maximize your time with the children while minimizing your spouse's time. Although you do want the court to create a schedule that gives you as much time as you need with your children, you also have to think about what's best for your children. They need a balanced, stable, and relatively stress-free life.

Before the divorce, your children lived in a home with two parents and had contact with both of them. Now that you and your spouse live in two separate homes, your children should continue receiving the emotional and financial support they have grown accustomed to.

Children also need a sense of normalcy and a schedule. How rigid this schedule needs to be depends on their age. In general, the older the child, the more flexible you can be. It's important to develop and follow a plan that allows your child time with each of you on a regular basis because children need a schedule to rely on. At the same time, parents need to be flexible to accommodate each other's schedules and their children's schedules and needs.

This chapter helps you create an accurate record of how you and your spouse are sharing your time with your children during the divorce. As you read, keep in mind that the whole point of a parenting plan is to allow children to spend time with both parents. Instead of trying to cut your spouse out of the picture, think about persuading the court to create a schedule that allows your child time with each of you. You may have different viewpoints about what is sensible and fair, but it's important that you approach the issue with that mind-set.

Some states no longer use the words *custody* and *visitation* because they have negative connotations. After all, no one truly "owns" a child, and a parent doesn't "visit" with a child. The prevailing thinking in the children's rights field is to refer to "parenting plans," "access," or "parenting time." Most parents, however, still think in terms of custody and visitation.

Creating an Accurate Visitation Record

While your case is pending, you probably will have a temporary order from the court describing a basic parenting schedule. In cases where the parents are able to work things out, a court will simply order "visitation at times as agreed," which gives you the flexibility to create a schedule that fits both of your needs. Either way, it's important that you keep an accurate record of when you each spend time with your children. Use your master calendar from Chapter 1 for this purpose.

When you get the temporary order describing when visitation is going to occur, record the schedule on your calendar. If the children are going to reside primarily with you, mark the times that they are to be with the other parent. If you are the parent with visitation, mark the times that are yours to spend with the children.

Some parents create a separate visitation calendar that shows each parent's time with different color markers. These calendars show you at a glance where the children will be, and they are easy for young children to understand. If you do use a separate calendar like this, make sure you go back and change it to reflect what actually happened (since schedules often get rearranged) so you have an accurate record of how time was spent with the children.

Visitation Issues to Record

There are several kinds of visitation situations you'll want to keep accurate records of.

Late Pickups or Drop-Offs

Pay attention to pickup and drop-off times. If your spouse is late picking up the child for his or her visit or is late bringing the child to you for your visit, make a note of it. Five minutes isn't important, but a half hour is. It might seem picky to write down actual pickup and drop-off times, but single instances can develop into larger patterns, and if you keep track of them you will have an accurate record of the problem.

Missed Visits

If your spouse forgets or cancels a scheduled visit with your children, note it on your calendar. Everyone forgets things once in a while, and situations arise that require us to cancel plans, but if this becomes a habit, you'll want a clear record of when and how often it happened. Children need routine, and if your spouse can't stick to one, you might use this information to persuade the court to cut back on his or her visitation time. On the flip side, if a parent doesn't spend time with the children, you can't force him or her to use visitation time, but you must continue to make that time available to him or her or you will violate the court order. You can point out how upsetting it is for the children and encourage him or her to show up when planned. Missed visits can be powerful evidence to refute a request for custody.

If you are the parent with visitation time and your spouse is canceling your visits, forgetting about them, or simply not allowing you access to the children, make sure you record these problems and discuss them with your attorney. Interference with visitation can be the basis for a change in custody. You don't want to encounter a situation where your spouse tells the court you're the one who didn't show up, so write down the times you came to pick up your child and note what happened.

Changes in Visitation

Some change to the parenting schedule is inevitable. You, your spouse, and your children all have busy lives, and things are bound to pop up now and then. If you agree to changes, make sure you record them on your calendar, and try to distribute the visits so that everyone gets a fair amount of time. For example, it's common for parents to alternate weekends:

Weekend 1: Parent A
Weekend 2: Parent B
Weekend 3: Parent A
Weekend 4: Parent B
Weekend 5: Parent A

When weekends are switched, the result can seem unfair. The visitation schedule could end up like this if the parents swapped Weekend 2 with Weekend 5:

Weekend 1: Parent A
Weekend 2: Parent A
Weekend 3: Parent A
Weekend 4: Parent B
Weekend 5: Parent B

The revised format doesn't feel as fair as the original one, but it still gives each parent the same amount of time. Writing it down can put everyone at ease that time is still fairly distributed.

When you agree to a change in visitation, record it on your calendar. Note the date it was changed from and which of you requested the change. If you get to a point where your spouse is requesting constant changes, you'll be able to show this pattern to the court. Constant changes can be upsetting to children, especially when they are first adjusting to a visitation schedule and the concept of divorce. Constant changes are also a sign that the current visitation plan is not working and may need to be modified.

Documenting Shared Custody

In most situations, judges identify one home that will be the child's primary residence and set up times when the nonresidential parent will have access. But in some situations, the court divides the child's time equally between the parents, giving neither one real residential custody. This arrangement is called joint, shared, or split custody. It might entail a child spending one week with one parent, the next week with the other, or half the week with one parent and half with the other. On rare occasions, time could be divided monthly.

If you and your spouse have shared custody, you'll want to keep a clear record of where your child is each day for your own scheduling reasons and to create documentation for the court. Record changes, tardiness, and missed days on the calendar.

Monitoring Your Children's Responses to Visitation

Throughout your case, pay attention to how your child is reacting to the parenting access schedule. Keep in mind that a new schedule, a divorce, and one parent moving into a new home are huge changes for children. Expect them to have trouble getting used to it all. Most parents are alarmed at the way their children react to divorce, and sometimes the knee-jerk response is to blame the other parent.

While it's important to keep an eye on your child's reactions, don't read too much into them. For example, if your child cries or screams each time he or she goes with the other parent, your first inclination might be that your spouse is doing something to cause this. Most of the time, the child is just reacting to the stress of the situation and to the emotions of the parents.

But sometimes the problem goes deeper than that. Sometimes an arrangement just isn't working for a child. The emphasis in these situations should be on finding solutions, not on pointing fingers. Some children, for example, have a hard time with transitions. Changing the time or location of the transition can help a lot in these situations. Other kids might resent having to miss soccer practice or Girl Scouts to go with a parent for a scheduled visit. Try to adjust the schedule around the children's needs. If your spouse is not cooperating, you need to document that for the court.

What seems like a crisis to you and your child may not seem so serious to a judge who has seen hundreds of children react to divorce. They don't have an easy time of it, but most children do adjust eventually. The court is not going to change custody or alter visitation simply because your child is having a hard time adjusting. You need to present persistent, ongoing reactions that clearly point to a problem. Keep detailed notes on the Children's Reactions Log at the end of this chapter.

If your child is having trouble handling the situation, a therapist can help him or her work through the confused emotions associated with the divorce and all of the changes it brings.

Children's Preferences

Courts pay attention to children's preferences about where they want to live when the children are in their preteen or teenage years. Although they may have strong preferences, younger children aren't given as much of a say. A child's maturity level is a factor in custody decisions.

As mentioned in Chapters 3 and 5, no matter what your child's age, he or she will probably have a law guardian or guardian ad litem—an attorney appointed by the court to represent him or her throughout the case. This lawyer meets with the children to find out how they feel about living arrangements and schedules.

Parents should not try to influence their children's opinions. Don't panic if your young child doesn't want to live with you. The judge and the law guardian are not going to base their decisions on that. They understand that children go through different phases while coping with divorce, and this involves frequent switching of loyalties. The court will take into consideration the opinions of teenagers who have a distinct preference about where they want to live, so listen to them and treat them with respect, even if you might not agree.

Grandparent Visitation

More and more courts are recognizing the importance of grandparents in a child's life. Although grandparents' rights are limited in some states, courts in other states will include provisions for grandparents to have access to their grandchildren in a divorce decree. Usually the noncustodial parent's parents are the ones who are given formal access to the children, since it is assumed that the custodial parent can assure his or her own parents of access. For example, if Mom has residential custody and Dad has visitation, the children will probably see Mom's parents on a regular basis, since they will spend most of their time with Mom. However, because Dad's time is limited, his parents might want the court to give them their own designated time with the children. If the noncustodial parent has limited access to the children, the court will want to make sure that the grandparents on that side of the family have access to the children.

If you oppose access by your in-laws, you'll need to document why you don't want your children to spend time with them. Keep notes about your children's visits with them and list any problems that have occurred. You'll want to document late pickups or drop-offs as well as missed visits. Use the Grandparent Visitation Log at the end of this chapter to record that information.

If you are arguing for your own parents to have access to your children, keep notes that record how the time is spent when the children are there, how the children enjoy their time with their grandparents, and how your spouse tries to interfere with or prevent the visits.

CHILDREN'S REACTIONS LOG

Make copies of this log for further use.

Date	Description

GRANDPARENT VISITATION LOG ▶

Name of grandparents _____

List the reasons you are opposed to visitation with these grandparents.

_____

_____

_____

_____

_____

_____

Create a log of problems that occur with grandparent visitation.

Date	Description

◀15▶

Witnesses and Evidence

Witnesses can be some of the most helpful types of evidence presented in a divorce, particularly with regard to custody. A custody decision is based on many subjective factors, such as a judge's perception, values, and opinions. Because judges in most states base their decisions on what is in the best interest of the child, and because witnesses are considered less biased than the parents, the court's decision will rely heavily on witnesses and their credibility. Witnesses can literally make or break your bid for custody. They can also provide important information for other parts of your case that don't deal with custody.

This chapter assists you in finding witnesses and summarizing how they can help your case. It also offers advice on preparing your own testimony. Doing these things for yourself will reduce the time your attorney needs to spend interviewing potential witnesses and preparing for the case.

Why You Need Witnesses

Witnesses present facts, opinions, and observations to the judge. If you testify that your spouse hit your child or withdrew all the money from your savings account, the judge will certainly consider your statement. However, if your neighbor testifies that she saw your spouse hit your child for spilling a cup of juice on the patio or that she heard your spouse talk about withdrawing all the money from your savings account, the judge will give more credence to her testimony because she is perceived as having no vested interest in the proceedings.

Witnesses are also important because trials can be boring. A sheaf of papers may give the judge enough evidence to support your position, but live testimony is much more compelling, and the judge is more likely to pay attention to it. Also, if the judge likes your witnesses, he or she is apt to like you. Remember, though, that the more witnesses your attorney presents, the longer the trial will last and the larger your legal bill will be. It's important that you and your attorney come up with enough witnesses to prove your case, but not so many that the proceedings become redundant and expensive.

Types of Witnesses to Find

Think about everything you are asking the court for. Then consider the people who will be able to offer facts or opinions that will convince the judge to give you what you want.

There are two types of witnesses: character witnesses and fact-based witnesses. Character witnesses are those who can say generally good things about you (or bad things about your spouse) and provide an overall description of what you are like as a person. These kinds of witnesses give information about overall character and personality. Character witnesses are important when custody is being determined, because they can impact the judge's impression of the parties. Character witnesses should be people who know you well and have known you for a long time, if possible. The same is true for character witnesses who point out negative qualities in your spouse.

Fact-based witnesses are those who can testify about things they know or saw. They are useful for any issue in a divorce.

Your attorney probably will not call all of the witnesses you've gathered, but it is helpful for him or her to have a list to work from. You want to give your attorney some choices to work with, because some witnesses will perform better than others. Some witnesses may be able to provide background information or documents that can be entered into evidence even if they don't testify, so don't leave them off your list.

Witness Characteristics

The best witnesses are those who can be objective—or at least *appear* objective. While your mother and brother may be able to testify about what a fantastic parent you are, the judge will understand that they have a vested interest in the case. If a close relative is the only one who can provide certain information, it is better to have the relative testify than no one at all.

You want your witnesses to be upstanding citizens whenever possible. Witnesses who are employed, have a stable lifestyle, have no criminal history or substance abuse problems, and have been decent people for most of their lives will do you the most good. You don't need Mary Poppins, but you want to avoid someone your spouse's attorney can turn the tables on during cross-examination. Don't worry about trying to find the perfect witnesses—your attorney will be able to work around their imperfections. Focus on coming up with credible people who can provide the best information to help your case.

Hearsay

Witnesses must have personal knowledge of the things they testify to. The hearsay rule, which prohibits people from testifying about things they do not have personal knowledge or experience with, must be taken into consideration when choosing your witnesses. For example, a witness can testify that he saw your spouse win $20,000 at a casino, but he cannot testify that his coworker saw this and then told him about it. He can't be sure it's true if he didn't see it for himself. If you have a doubt as to whether a witness would be able to testify about something, include him or her on your list and let your attorney decide.

Subject Matter for Witness Testimony

The following are examples of the types of witnesses you will need for the various issues being dealt with in your divorce.

Alimony

- professionals such as office managers, human resource employees, or business partners who can provide proof of your or your spouse's income, assets, expenses, and any unreported income (if there is no documentary evidence)
- people who have direct knowledge of "bad behavior," such as infidelity, by one of the spouses; police reports about domestic violence (In some states, bad behavior can influence the amount or length of alimony.)
- professionals who can support or refute career or education needs and expenses after divorce for the spouse who is seeking alimony (e.g., an employer or a college career counselor)

Child Support

- people who can provide proof of your or your spouse's income or assets or who have information about unreported income (if there is no documentary evidence), such as office managers, human resource personnel, business partners, or bank personnel
- experts who can support or refute testimony about special needs your child has, such as physical therapists, physicians, mental health therapists, or teachers

Property and Debt Division

- an expert who can value a business or license
- family members, business associates, and others who have information about assets that your spouse has allegedly hidden or stolen

- lenders who can testify about debts you or your spouse have incurred (if there is no documentary evidence), such as family members or friends you have borrowed from
- experts who can value real estate, jewelry, or any special collections

Custody

- teachers who can talk about parental involvement and the child's needs
- therapists, psychologists, or doctors who can discuss a child's special needs, parental involvement, and family dynamics
- therapists or psychologists who can evaluate your and your spouse's abilities

- friends, neighbors, or family members who can cite specific instances that demonstrate each spouse's parenting skills and fitness or unfitness

Reason for Divorce
- for contested grounds (which is rare), witnesses who have knowledge of the reasons behind the breakup of the marriage

Your attorney will want to use documents to prove many financial facts, because it is faster and less expensive than bringing in live witnesses. Why have your bank manager testify about how much money is in your savings account when you can prove it with bank records? However, it is a good idea to include witnesses on your list who can back up the evidence in the documents in case of a dispute. The classic example of a witness who can back up the information in documentary evidence is the office manager or someone from your spouse's place of employment who can testify about the availability of overtime, your spouse's history of accepting overtime, and the fact that he or she has cut back on overtime since the divorce proceedings began—a tactic used to reduce income so that child support and alimony will be lower.

Preparing a Witness List

Once you have thought about the kind of information you need and the people who can provide it, complete the List of Possible Witnesses at the end of this chapter. Then fill out a Witness Worksheet for each person, also at the end of this chapter. Fill in the contact information at the top of the sheet, write down the facts the witness can share, and indicate if he or she can offer character evidence about you. Make note of important events he or she has witnessed. Take a few days to complete these worksheets, and jot down points as they come to mind. Although you want to organize your information logically, it's more important to get it all down than to have it in perfect form. Your attorney will create his or her own notes anyway.

It's permissible to talk to the people you put on your witness list to see if they remember what you remember. Tell them you want them to testify and that they need to speak with your attorney, but don't try to influence what they will say. You can add people to your witness list who are not willing to testify, if you believe they have information that will help your case. Don't try to talk to these people about what they know, though, because they could change their story or alert your spouse. Your attorney can subpoena them and require them to testify. Make sure you discuss these witnesses thoroughly with your attorney, because they might be upset that they have been subpoenaed. Never promise anyone anything in exchange for testimony.

Some witnesses may have documents or other types of evidence that could help your case. It is best if they give these items to your attorney directly, but if a witness insists on giving something to you, accept it and give it to your attorney.

Being Your Own Witness

Most parties to a divorce case end up testifying themselves. After all, you are the one who has the most information about your situation. When you testify, your job will be to answer the questions you are asked, first by your attorney and then by your spouse's attorney. Your attorney will help you prepare your testimony, but it is important to be truthful and to report things accurately.

To prepare yourself to testify, create a comprehensive list of events and facts that are essential to your case and about which you can provide information. Even if you have other witnesses who can testify, your attorney should have a complete list of what you can testify about. Your attorney will decide how to present the information. Use the Notes for Your Testimony worksheet at the end of this chapter. Work on it over a few days, jotting things down as they occur to you. Try to group your thoughts under the categories on the worksheet. If you're not sure where something goes, place it under "Other." Don't try to include all the details—just cover the key points. You can discuss the details with your attorney. Once you have written down everything you can remember, read it over and cross out things about which you do not have firsthand knowledge. This list will give your attorney an outline to use in preparing you for questioning.

Note that this form does not include a section for custody. See Chapter 16 for more information about preparing your testimony for a custody trial.

Preparing for Your Spouse's Witnesses

Your spouse will present witnesses in court, just as you do. After his or her attorney is done questioning them, your attorney will have the opportunity to do so. This is called *cross-examination*. It is your turn to get more information from the witnesses or to show that they are leaving facts out, not being truthful, or clouding the facts.

Take time to think about the witnesses your spouse will call. Sometimes attorneys exchange witness lists during the discovery phase, but this does not happen all of the time, or even most of the time. This is a choice your attorney will make. If they do exchange lists, ask your attorney for a copy of your spouse's witness list and use that when you prepare your cross-examination notes. If lists are not exchanged, you may hear through the grapevine or make some educated guesses about friends and relatives who have been subpoenaed or asked to testify. You can expect your spouse to testify as well. Prepare the Cross-Examination Notes worksheet at the end of the chapter by first filling in the names of witnesses you are sure will be called or who are on the witness list obtained by your attorney. Then write down what they know, how they can hurt your case (be honest here), things you know about them that make them look bad, and information they have that will be helpful to your case. It is important to be honest about what these witnesses know. You want your attorney to be prepared in the courtroom, not surprised.

Leave some of these pages blank and bring them to court with you in case your spouse calls any witnesses you did not anticipate. Use the pages to make notes of things they say that are not true, facts they leave out, and issues your attorney should ask about on cross-examination. The court might grant your attorney a few minutes to meet with you before cross-examining a surprise witness, and you can share the information then; if not, you can pass the pages to your attorney while he or she is questioning the witness.

Physical Evidence

If you've learned anything from this book, it's probably the fact that paperwork and documents are key to the divorce process. After all, you probably bought this book to help organize that paperwork. And as much as these documents are an important type of evidence, some cases require evidence beyond paper. The following sections will discuss the types of physical evidence (other than documents and papers) that you might need in your case. Create a list of evidence using the Physical Evidence List at the end of this chapter.

Photographs

Photographs can provide persuasive evidence. You might use them to show:

- your history as a parent (through a photo album)
- mistreatment of you or your child by your spouse
- conditions that exist in either home (e.g., mold, dirt, safety hazards, overcrowding)
- proof that certain assets or belongings exist
- value of some belongings or assets (a set of antique glass might sound expensive, but a photograph could show it to be chipped and cracked)
- damage done by your spouse to marital assets

Photographs can be compelling evidence, because they show the judge in full color what you are trying to prove. They offer clear visual images that often have more impact than testimony by a witness.

Photographs cannot be submitted to the court alone, however. In order to enter a photograph into evidence, your attorney must have the person who took the photos available to testify. The person who took the photo must testify that he or she took the photo, that it is an accurate representation of whatever it is showing, and that the photograph has not been altered.

If you have photographs to give your attorney, you can label them on the back, indicating when each was taken, by whom, and who or what is in it, or you can number the back of each photo and create a written list containing that same information. It is a good idea to keep copies of photographs because if they are entered into evidence, you may not get them back. You should also keep the negatives, if they exist. If it is a digital photo, keep the disk or memory stick.

Videotape

Videotape can be another compelling kind of evidence. Video can reveal a person's character or behavior in a way photographs cannot, because it shows the person in action. If you submit a video to your attorney, be sure to label it with the date and what it shows. If the video is something you want to keep, make a copy of it. Some courts will require testimony by the person who shot the tape or was in control of the video camera to ensure that the tape has not been tampered with.

Don't bother submitting a video unless it shows something important. A video of a child's dance recital or a birthday party won't impress a judge, but one that shows the way a parent treats a child or that captures a significant and revealing event could be useful in the case. If you have both photos and video, let your attorney know and he or she will select which to use.

Voice Recordings

Some people tape-record conversations with their spouses without realizing that it is illegal in many states to record another person without his or her permission. To find out what the laws are in your state, visit www.rcfp .org/taping or contact your attorney or state attorney general. When submitting recordings to your attorney, be sure to label the tapes with dates and the names of the people who are on the tapes. Voice recordings will be of interest only if they provide substantive evidence or an important admission by your spouse.

Other Physical Evidence

Other types of physical evidence your attorney might be able to use include:

- items damaged by your spouse
- ripped, filthy, or bloody clothing (yours or your child's) to show abuse or neglect
- computer disks
- computer file evidence of child pornography
- answering machine or voice mail messages

When presenting physical evidence, someone (you or another witness) with direct knowledge about the item must testify. When submitting physical evidence to your attorney, include a written explanation of what the item is, its significance, and who the appropriate witness might be.

How to Find Evidence

All the evidence you provide to your attorney must be tied to some issue in the case, so the first thing to think about is what you're trying to prove. Examples might include:

- Your spouse is a bad parent.
- You are a wonderful parent.
- Your child has special needs.
- Your spouse destroyed marital assets.
- Your spouse threatened you or harmed you.
- Your spouse is not fully disclosing income or assets.

Use the Physical Evidence List at the end of this chapter to clarify what each piece of evidence can prove about you or your spouse. Then gather the evidence you need when your spouse is not around. If you fear repercussions from your spouse, discuss your concerns with your attorney.

You can snoop around to find things that might help your case, but the final call as to whether something is useful should be left up to your attorney. Your job is to provide him or her with as much information and evidence as possible. Then stand aside as he or she decides what can legally be used and what fits into the strategy for the case.

LIST OF POSSIBLE WITNESSES

Name	Topics

WITNESS WORKSHEET

Create one worksheet for each witness.

Name _____

Age _____

Address _____

Phone _____

Employment _____

Relationship _____

Information witness can provide

_____

_____

_____

_____

_____

_____

_____

_____

_____

_____

_____

_____

_____

_____

_____

_____

NOTES FOR YOUR TESTIMONY ▶

Make notes on these pages about what you can testify to.

Alimony

_____

_____

_____

_____

_____

_____

Child Support

_____

_____

_____

_____

_____

_____

Property and Debt Division
(You do not need to re-create your list of disputed items from
Chapter 11. Instead, explain why you should get certain items.)

_____

_____

_____

_____

_____

Reason for Divorce

_____

_____

_____

_____

_____

_____

Other

_____

_____

_____

_____

_____

_____

_____

_____

_____

_____

_____

_____

_____

_____

_____

_____

CROSS-EXAMINATION NOTES

Make copies of this log for further use.

Witness's Name _____

_____

_____

_____

_____

_____

_____

_____

_____

_____

_____

_____

_____

_____

_____

_____

_____

_____

_____

_____

_____

_____

_____

_____

PHYSICAL EVIDENCE LIST

Make copies of this log for further use.

Description	What It Can Prove

16

Custody Trials

If you're going to have a trial about custody, prepare yourself for some serious mudslinging. This is often the nastiest, most painful, and most emotional part of a divorce trial. You and your spouse will each try to show the court that you are a terrific parent and that the other person is a terrible parent. Sometimes these trials involve big issues such as abuse or neglect, but most of the time they deal with tiny pieces—child care, day-to-day activities, and particular events—that can be painstaking to put together.

There are two types of custody trials. Some couples have similar ideas about how to arrange custody and visitation but simply can't agree on the details. This impasse sometimes leads to a visitation trial in which the emphasis is on schedules. Other couples have knock-down, drag-out custody battles in which each wants to be the residential parent. These cases involve a lot of evidence and testimony about parenting abilities and events.

This chapter helps you gather evidence and record situations so that your attorney can convince the court that your position on custody or visitation is the right one.

Documenting the Past

Although the court is going to place the most emphasis on the current parenting arrangement, the past is important, too. Most parents are on their best behavior while the case is pending, but you want to show what things were like before you came to court. Take some time to reconstruct what you can of the last few months or the last year. You may need to go even further back if something important occurred in the past—if you took a year off to be home with the kids, for example, or one of you missed a lot of time at work to care for a sick child. The distant past is relevant if it shows a significant commitment to your children or a significant failure by the other parent. Use your personal calendar or the family calendar for this purpose. Go through and highlight dates your spouse was out of town or worked long hours and could not spend time with the children. Highlight special events, recitals, sports events, and so on that he or she missed.

Documenting Your Own Parenting Abilities

It might seem difficult to take a step back and look objectively at your own parenting abilities, but you need to do so in order to build your case. Go through the calendar and make note of all the times you were there for your children—events, games, practices, doctor appointments, time off from work when they were sick, and so on. Fill in special little things you did with your kids: you might remember that you took them on a long bike ride over the Memorial Day weekend or that you went to a movie on a weeknight in January. Fill in what you can recall.

Continue to keep accurate records about parenting. Your calendar will be your essential tool for doing this. Record every activity you participate in with your children. Record times you drive them places. Make notes about different places you take them or major things you do together.

Use the Child Care Checklist at the end of this chapter to document the things you usually do for your child. The list can be persuasive if you are trying to convince your spouse that you should have residential custody, and it is helpful for your attorney. Check off the things that you routinely do or supervise as a parent. Leave blank those items that usually apply to your spouse. Cross off items that do not apply to your child (such as diapers if your children are older or activities that no longer require your supervision). If some things are shared equally, place a *J* next to them. Then look at the list. If you have checked most of the items, then you are the one who has been primarily involved in day-to-day care of your child. If most items have a *J*, then you and your spouse have truly been equal partners in parenting and a joint parenting arrangement might work best. If you have left most items blank, it means your spouse has done most of the day-to-day child care and supervision. This doesn't mean you can't get custody of your child, but it does mean that the family is more accustomed to your spouse handling the daily arrangements. You should probably not give this checklist to your attorney if it does not show you taking on most of the child care responsibilities. However, if you are only seeking visitation and your spouse is opposing it, a checklist that shows moderate involvement can be helpful.

If parenting responsibilities have changed, make a note of this in the margin of the checklist. For example, perhaps you drove your child to elementary school every day for six years, but he or she now walks to middle school. Or maybe you are the parent of a two-year-old who recently became potty trained, but you are the one who was primarily responsible for diapers and potty training. These notes can help your attorney see a pattern of who is taking on parenting responsibilities.

Focusing on the Other Parent's Faults

If you're going to win a custody case, you've got to present the other parent in a way that convinces the judge that you are the person the child should spend most of his or her time with. This doesn't mean complete character assassination, but it does mean you need to document anything that negatively impacts your spouse's parenting abilities. Of course, you should never set out to prove something that you know isn't true.

In pointing out your spouse's shortcomings, focus on points that affect his or her parenting abilities rather than general lifestyle issues. Many parents, for example, are quick to point out that their spouse has a new girlfriend or boyfriend. In actuality, the court is interested in this new partner only if the relationship has a negative impact on the children. If the children don't have much contact with the new partner, or if they do see the person a lot but it's not a negative situation, the court won't care. The judge doesn't care if your spouse is a lying, scheming rat toward you as long as he or she is not that way with the children. His or her personality traits, lifestyle choices, and actions matter only if they have a negative impact on the children.

Use the Spouse's Parenting Abilities form at the end of this chapter to write down incidents that demonstrate the problems your spouse has as a parent. While your take on the situation is important, think about other people who can second your opinion. Are there friends, relatives, or neighbors who have observed the behaviors that you noted? See Chapter 15 for more information about compiling a witness list.

Parenting Classes

Some courts routinely refer parents to classes or seminars on how to get along after a divorce and how to manage visitation. If you are referred to this kind of program, go even if your spouse is not going. Your attendance is reported to the court and will cast you in a better light.

If there is a question about one parent's ability to care for children, the court might order him or her to attend a parenting skills class. If this happens to you, don't be insulted—think of it as an opportunity to show the court that you are reliable, trustworthy, proactive, and responsible. If you are adamant about not partaking in these classes, the alternative is to have your attorney obtain a professional evaluation of your parenting skills (which you will have to pay for) by a psychologist or therapist. This professional will provide a report that the court will rely upon.

If you believe your spouse seriously lacks parenting skills, talk to your attorney about requesting classes for him or her.

Keeping Your Kids Out of It

It is tempting to rely on information you get from your child to help you win a custody case, but that information is often unreliable. Parents get upset when a child returns from the other parent's home and tells them about what they did, what the parent did or said, or problems that occurred. Remember that your child will almost always try to play one parent against the other and will be encouraged by your obvious reactions. He or she wants to please you or get a reaction out of you, and if telling you unflattering things about the other parent accomplishes that, he or she will continue to do so and may even make things up. If you've ever heard your child describe an event that you attended, you know that children usually don't report accurately. When your child tells it, facts that you think are important to the narrative are often left out, and minor details become important parts of the story.

It is tempting to pump your child for information after he or she spends time with the other parent, but it's a bad idea. Although you are trying to build your case, you have to respect your child's right to a relationship with the other parent. Your child is not a spy for either of you, and placing him or her in that position can only be damaging.

That being said, sometimes there are things you learn from your child that you just can't ignore. If your child comes home and tells you "Mommy hit me" or "Daddy wouldn't let me go to my basketball game," you know there's a problem. The key here is to not jump to conclusions. You're probably not getting the full story from your child. There are probably details left out that could change your take on it. Consider asking the other parent about what happened. If you're satisfied with his or her explanation, let it go. If you're not satisfied, or if these situations occur repeatedly and your spouse has an excuse for every one, it's time to create a record.

Keep a Parenting Journal to record things your child tells you, things your spouse tells you, and things you notice yourself. You can use the page at the end of this chapter or buy a separate journal.

Siblings and Half Siblings

Your child's relationships with siblings are an important part of his or her life. While it is very rare for a court to separate siblings, a judge might consider a spouse's suggestion to split them up. If you are worried about it, take steps to document how important the children are to each other. Use your Parenting Journal to record how they spend their time together and how they relate to each other.

If you have children from a prior marriage or relationship, these half siblings are equally important in your child's life. If the half siblings are with you only part of the time (because of the parenting plan you have with the other parent), create a clear schedule so you can ensure that the court-appointed visitation schedule allows the children of this marriage time together with their half siblings. Again, you should document the time they spend together, what they do together, and how important they are to each other.

CHILD CARE CHECKLIST ▶

Use this checklist to document things you usually do for your child.

1. Hygiene

☐ baths

☐ cleaning hands and face

☐ brushing teeth

☐ flossing

☐ diaper changes/bathroom use

☐ hair combing/styling

☐ nail care

☐ cleaning up child after meals

☐ haircuts

☐ dressing

☐ laundry

☐ changing sheets

☐ purchasing clothing and shoes

☐ child's room cleaning

☐ child's bathroom cleaning

2. Meals and Food

☐ feeding

☐ preparation

☐ cleanup

☐ planning

☐ shopping

☐ snacks

☐ packing lunches

☐ preparing and sending food items to school (birthday, parties, etc.)

☐ teaching child to cook

3. Sleep

☐ bedtime rituals

☐ nighttime wake-ups

☐ naps

☐ morning wake-ups

4. Education

☐ reading to the child

☐ help with homework

☐ parent-teacher conferences

☐ attending school functions

4. Education (continued)

- [ ] doing educational activities at home
- [ ] transportation to/from school
- [ ] transportation to/from activities
- [ ] child care when home sick
- [ ] arrangements for extracurriculars, sports, and so on
- [ ] driver education
- [ ] parental attendance at extra-curriculars, sports, and so on
- [ ] parental involvement in extra-curriculars, sports, and so on
- [ ] offering explanations
- [ ] trips to the library
- [ ] trips to museums and other educational places
- [ ] arts and crafts projects
- [ ] homeschooling

5. Emotional Nurturing

- [ ] rocking, soothing, holding
- [ ] talks and advice
- [ ] participating in child's interests
- [ ] comforting
- [ ] humor
- [ ] self-esteem
- [ ] setting and enforcing rules and limits

6. Health Care

- [ ] taking child to health care appointments
- [ ] scheduling health care appointments
- [ ] giving/supervising medication
- [ ] home medical care (cuts, stings, scrapes, headaches)
- [ ] calling health care providers for assistance
- [ ] sunscreen application
- [ ] bug repellent application
- [ ] bicycle helmet

7. Entertainment and Play

☐ driving child to parties, play dates

☐ supervising friends at home

☐ playing sports with child

☐ watching TV/videos with child

☐ playing games

☐ playing with toys

☐ buying toys

☐ organizing toys

☐ planning family vacations

☐ party planning

☐ purchasing gifts for the child

☐ assisting child with pet care

SPOUSE'S PARENTING ABILITIES

Use this form to record actual incidents or general impressions of your spouse's parenting.

_____
_____
_____
_____
_____
_____
_____
_____
_____
_____
_____
_____
_____
_____
_____
_____
_____
_____
_____
_____
_____
_____
_____
_____
_____
_____

PARENTING JOURNAL

Use this form to record impressions about custody and visitation, things your child or spouse might say, and details about what happened on certain days or in certain situations that might support your position on custody and visitation.

_____

_____

_____

_____

_____

_____

_____

_____

_____

_____

_____

_____

_____

_____

_____

_____

_____

_____

_____

_____

_____

_____

17

It's All Over! Now What?

Once your divorce is official, there will be loose ends to tie up and things you'll need to continue tracking. Your divorce is finalized once your attorney has filed or recorded the papers. It may take a week or two after the judge's decision for it to be official.

Changing Your Name

Your divorce decree will include authorization to change your name. Once the decree is final, you may resume using your premarital name or you can continue using your marital name if you wish. This is a matter of personal choice. You will need to show a copy of your divorce decree and marriage license when changing your name on official documents such as a driver's license, passport, or social security card. Your new driver's license will usually suffice as proof for other documents that require a name change. Use this checklist to ensure you changed your name in all the essential places:

☐ auto insurance
☐ bank accounts
☐ car registration

- [ ] catalogs
- [ ] children's schools or day care
- [ ] club or gym memberships
- [ ] credit cards
- [ ] dental insurance
- [ ] driver's license (check your state department of motor vehicles website for forms and information)
- [ ] dry cleaner
- [ ] employer (get a new ID card if your employer requires one)
- [ ] frequent-flier programs
- [ ] health care providers (for you and your children)
- [ ] health insurance (get a new card)
- [ ] investments
- [ ] library card
- [ ] life insurance
- [ ] newspaper and magazine subscriptions
- [ ] passport (visit http://travel.state.gov/get_forms.html)
- [ ] pensions and retirement plans
- [ ] social security card (visit www.ssa.gov/replace_sscard/html)
- [ ] utility bills
- [ ] union
- [ ] veterinarian

Updating Your Insurance

Remove your ex-spouse from your auto and home owner's or renter's insurance policies. Make sure your policy now covers only the vehicle or property that is in your name and that your name is not on the policy for items your ex-spouse now owns. Change the beneficiary of your life insurance policy if it is currently your spouse (unless the court has ordered you to continue it). Most people name their children when changing this.

If you will be receiving health insurance through your spouse's plan under COBRA (a federal law permitting you to pay for your own continuing coverage through the plan for eighteen months after a divorce), complete the paperwork required by the carrier and find out how much the premiums will be and when they will be due each month. Ask if they will send you a bill or if you are responsible for making payments on your own. Mark the due dates on your calendar. Find out when you are no longer eligible for COBRA coverage and mark that date on your calendar as well. Also make a note to yourself six months before that date to start seeking new coverage. It's important to do this well in advance, because most health care plans have enrollment periods only two to four times a year.

Protecting Your Credit

Make sure that you have closed or frozen all joint credit cards. Open new accounts in your own name. Obtain a copy of your credit report about three to five months after the divorce is finalized and check for joint accounts. If any still appear on the report, close them in writing. Some accounts that you closed might still appear as open on your report. Contact the credit reporting agency and ask that their status be changed.

Dividing Assets

When your divorce is finalized, you'll get directives on how everything is to be divided between you and your ex-spouse. If you still have personal property that belongs to each other, you'll want to exchange it as soon as possible. If your ex-spouse is not cooperative, let your attorney know. He or she will contact your ex-spouse's attorney to make sure it gets done. Use the Receipts for Property Distribution at the end of this chapter to keep track of what has been exchanged.

You'll also need to get ownership changed on larger items that were owned jointly and will now be in your name alone. For cars and boats you'll need a copy of the title and of the divorce decree. Contact your state department of motor vehicles for title transfer information. Houses are more complicated. You can get the deed changed, but changing the mortgage will usually require you to refinance it in the name of the person who is the sole owner. When dealing with bank accounts and investments, it is simplest to close the joint account and roll the money into single accounts.

Leases

If you and your ex-spouse rented your residence and you are now the sole occupant of the apartment, contact your landlord and amend the lease to include only your name. Leaving your ex's name on the lease will make him or her responsible for rent (which might not bother you), but it will also give him or her the legal right to access the apartment (something you don't want). If you are moving out, be sure you're no longer financially responsible for rent.

Your Will

Once your divorce is final, you will need to change your will. If you had a will while you were married, it probably named your ex-spouse as a beneficiary. You probably want to change that now. Think carefully about how you would like to distribute your belongings. If you have children and you are the parent they primarily live with, you will need to name a guardian for them in case you die while they are still minors and you do not want your ex to have custody. In the event of your death, the court will consider your choice but will make the final decision. Preference is usually given to the other parent unless there is a very good reason not to.

Health Care Directives

If you have not already done so, make sure you change your health care directives so that your ex-spouse no longer has the ability to make decisions for you if you are ill and can't decide for yourself.

Wedding and Relationship Mementos

Now that your marriage is over, you probably have mixed feelings about things like your wedding photos, wedding ring, and keepsakes. Some people feel the need to get rid of it all. Others recognize that these things represent happy times (even if they didn't last) and are an important part of their personal history. However you feel about it, it is your choice and there is no wrong answer.

If you have children, consider their feelings about these items. Your marriage is important to them and they might want to have your wedding photos, dress, or rings sometime in the future. Photographs of their parents together will have meaning to them because these are part of their family history.

If you do decide to get rid of things like your wedding ring or dress, consider reselling them to make some extra cash. Some women have the diamond from their engagement ring reset as a pendant or earrings.

Coping with Your Feelings

When your divorce becomes final, you will probably experience a wide range of feelings, including relief, sadness, joy, depression, independence, anger, resentment, or grief. All of these reactions are normal, and your feelings will probably change as you move along. Your reaction to your divorce doesn't end with the final decision in the case. Adjusting to a different life is a long and difficult process, and you shouldn't feel that you need to follow a timetable. Many people find that the actual divorce process kept their mind occupied and that the post-divorce period is unexpectedly more difficult. Don't be afraid to seek counseling if you need it.

Continuing to Track Payments

You will need to continue tracking child support and alimony payments. Make copies of the Ongoing Child Support Log and the Ongoing Alimony Log at the end of this chapter and complete them regularly. Also make copies of the Child Support and Alimony Receipts and use them for ongoing payments.

When you transfer property or assets according to the divorce decree, get a receipt for items that will not leave a paper trail on their own. For example, when you roll a mutual fund from joint names to your ex-spouse, there is a record of this. But when you give your ex $500 cash or expensive photography equipment, there will not be a paper trail unless you create one. Ask your ex-spouse to sign a receipt indicating acceptance of the item. Use the receipts at the end of this chapter.

Maintaining Your Household

Whether you are remaining in the marital home after a divorce or are moving to a new residence, you have to take stock of your household. Lots of things have changed, and this is a time for reassessment.

Now that you have physically separated and divided your possessions, one of the first things you need to do is assess what you've got and what you need. It's easy to think of all the things you jointly owned as being around for your use, but when you can't find that serving dish, CD, or screwdriver you need, you realize that things have changed. It can be expensive to reequip your household. Try these money-saving ideas:

- Go to yard sales or garage sales.
- Visit secondhand stores.
- Ask friends and relatives for things they don't want.
- Shop sales and warehouse clubs.
- Watch for sales, discounts, and rebates.
- Compare prices.
- Shop on eBay.
- Don't replace things unless you really need them.

You'll find that once you are on your own, you can change many things about the way you live since you have no one to answer to but yourself. Try out new things and new routines. Many people discover surprising new things about themselves after divorce.

Managing Finances

You now have the freedom to change not only how you live, but also how you manage your finances. You are now solely responsible for all spending and earning in your household. This can be a burden or a great freedom. Learn to budget your money and your expenses so that you have a clear idea of how much you can spend. Once you adjust to the new order, start thinking about the future. You are now completely responsible for your own retirement, so start thinking about how you will manage it.

When you file your taxes, you can file as single or as single head of household for the first calendar year you are not married. Before then, you will need to consult your tax advisor about how you will file for the calendar year that you were married and then divorced in. Make sure you are clear as to whether you or your ex-spouse will be claiming the children, as discussed in Chapter 12.

Important Documents for Your Child

If you are the parent with residential custody, make sure you are in possession of the following items for each child:

- birth certificate
- baptismal certificate (if any)
- passport
- social security card
- bank statements for accounts in the child's name
- life insurance policies
- immunization records
- important medical records
- health insurance cards

If you do not have residential custody of your children, make sure you:

- Contact your children's schools and the leaders of their extracurricular activities and arrange to receive separate copies of report cards, notices, calendars, and schedules for parent-teacher conferences.

- Notify your children's medical care providers that you have the authority to seek treatment for your child (you may need to provide copies of your custody papers), and arrange for separate updates on your child's health if necessary. If you do not have joint legal custody, your ex may need to complete an authorization allowing you to obtain care when the child is with you.
- Keep copies of the child's health insurance card, birth certificate, and social security card.

RECEIPTS FOR PROPERTY DISTRIBUTION

Make copies of these receipts so you can fill them out whenever property is exchanged.

Property Receipt

I received the following item _____ from

_____ on _____ (date) as part of the property distribution agreement order.

_____
(signature)

Property Receipt

I received the following item _____ from

_____ on _____ (date) as part of the property distribution agreement order.

_____
(signature)

Property Receipt

I received the following item _____ from

_____ on _____ (date) as part of the property distribution agreement order.

_____
(signature)

Property Receipt

I received the following item _____ from

_____ on _____ (date) as part of the property distribution agreement order.

_____
(signature)

ONGOING CHILD SUPPORT LOG

Make copies of this log so you can continue to track child support payments.

Date	Check Number	Amount	Payment Period	Check if Unpaid

CHILD SUPPORT RECEIPTS

Make several copies of this page so that you can prepare a receipt for each month.

Child Support Receipt

I received $_____ from _____ on _____ (date)

for the period of _____ to _____ as child support.

_____
(signature)

Child Support Receipt

I received $_____ from _____ on _____ (date)

for the period of _____ to _____ as child support.

_____
(signature)

Child Support Receipt

I received $_____ from _____ on _____ (date)

for the period of _____ to _____ as child support.

_____
(signature)

Child Support Receipt

I received $_____ from _____ on _____ (date)

for the period of _____ to _____ as child support.

_____
(signature)

ONGOING ALIMONY LOG

Make copies of this log so you can continue to track alimony payments.

Date	Check Number	Amount	Payment Period	Check if Unpaid

ALIMONY RECEIPTS

Make copies of this page so you can fill out a receipt for every payment.

Alimony Receipt

I received $_____ from _____ on _____ (date)

for the period of _____ to _____ as alimony.

_____
(signature)

Alimony Receipt

I received $_____ from _____ on _____ (date)

for the period of _____ to _____ as alimony.

_____
(signature)

Alimony Receipt

I received $_____ from _____ on _____ (date)

for the period of _____ to _____ as alimony.

_____
(signature)

Alimony Receipt

I received $_____ from _____ on _____ (date)

for the period of _____ to _____ as alimony.

_____
(signature)

Appendix
Resources

Organizations

American Academy of Matrimonial Lawyers
150 N. Michigan Ave., Suite 2040
Chicago, IL 60601
312-263-6477
www.aaml.org

American Association for Marriage and Family Therapy
112 S. Alfred St.
Alexandria, VA 22314-3061
703-838-9808
www.aamft.org

American Bar Association
740 15th St., NW
Washington, DC 20005-1019
202-662-1000
www.abanet.org

American Counseling Association
5999 Stevenson Ave.
Alexandria, VA 22304
800-347-6647
www.counseling.org

American Psychological Association
750 First St., NE
Washington, DC 20002-4242
800-374-2721
www.apa.org

Association for Conflict Resolution
1015 18th St., NW, Suite 1150
Washington, DC 20036
202-464-9700
www.acresolution.org

Banana Splits (children's divorce support)
53 Columbus Ave., #2
New York, NY 10023
212-262-4562

Children's Rights Council
6200 Editors Park Dr., Suite 103
Hyattsville, MD 20782
301-559-3120
www.gocrc.org

Coalition for Collaborative Divorce
PMB 623
23679 Calabasas Rd.
Calabasas, CA 91302-1502
800-559-3724
www.nocourtdivorce.com

Equifax (credit reporting agency)
P.O. Box 740241
Atlanta, GA 30374
800-685-1111
www.equifax.com

Experian (credit reporting agency)
P.O. Box 2104
Allen, TN 75013-2104
888-397-3742
www.experian.com

National Child Support Enforcement Association
444 North Capitol St., Suite 414
Washington, DC 20001-1512
202-624-8180
www.ncsea.org

National Family Resiliency Center, Inc.
(formerly Children of Separation and Divorce Center)
2000 Century Plaza, Suite 121
Columbia, MD 21044
410-740-9553
www.divorceabc.com

Parents Without Partners
1650 Dixie Highway, Suite 510
Boca Raton, FL 33432
561-391-8833
www.parentswithoutpartners.org

Trans Union (credit reporting agency)
Consumer Disclosure Center
P.O. Box 1000
Chester, PA 19022
www.tuc.com

Websites

American Responsible Divorce Network: www.responsible-divorce.com
Appraiser USA: http://appraiserusa.com (home appraisal)
Better Divorce: www.betterdivorce.com
Budgeting: www.betterbudgeting.com
Business evaluation: www.bulletproofbizplans.com/BallPark
Calendar maker: www.calendarhome.com
Car Blue Book value: www.kbb.com
Child support arrears calculator:
   www.childsupport.com/calculator.asp
Child support calculators by state:
   www.alllaw.com/calculators/childsupport
Children and divorce:
   www.hec.ohio-state.edu/famlife/divorce/pguides/intro.htm
Children and divorce research: www.bol.ucla.edu/~jeffwood
Choosing a child therapist:
   http://kidshealth.org/parent/emotions/feelings/finding_therapist.html
Choosing a therapist: http://psychcentral.com/therapst.htm
Divorce Care: www.divorcecare.com
Divorce Central: www.divorcecentral.com
Divorce and Children: www.divorceandchildren.com
Divorce Doc: www.divorcedoc.com
Divorce Help www.divorcehelp.com
DivorceNet: www.divorcenet.com
Divorce Online: www.divorceonline.com
Divorce Plus: http://pages.prodigy.com/divorceplus/divcont.htm
Divorce Recovery: www.divorcerecovery101.com
Divorce Source: www.divorcesource.com
Divorce Support: www.divorcesupport.com
Domestic violence: www.ncadv.org
Effects of divorce on children:
   www.hec.ohio-state.edu/famlife/divorce/effects.htm
Federal Office of Child Support Enforcement:
   www.acf.dhhs.gov/programs/cse
Moving: www.moving.org
Moving: www.usps.com/moversguide

Realtor Finder: www.realtorfinder.com
Separated Parenting Access and Resource Center:
   www.deltabravo.net/custody
Single Parent Central: www.singleparentcentral.com
Single parent network: www.makinglemonade.com
Single Parents: www.singleparents.about.com
Smart Divorce: www.smartdivorce.com
State Bar Association links:
   www.findlaw.com/06associations/state.html
State divorce laws: www.findlaw.com
Surviving Divorce: www.survive-divorce.com

Magazines

Divorce Magazine: www.divorcemag.com

Books for Parents

The Best Parent Is Both Parents: A Guide to Shared Parenting in the 21st Century by David L. Levy (Hampton Roads, 1993).

Caught in the Middle: Protecting the Children of High-Conflict Divorce by Carla B. Garrity (Jossey-Bass, 1997).

Collecting Child Support by Suzan Herskowitz (Made E-Z, 2001).

The Complete Divorce Recovery Handbook by John P. Splinter (Zondervan, 1992).

Co-Parenting After Divorce: How to Raise Happy, Healthy Children in Two-Home Families by Diana Shulman (Winnspeed Press, 1997).

Crazy Time: Surviving Divorce and Building a New Life by Abigail Trafford (Perennial, 1992).

Divorce: Six Ways to Get Through the Bad Times for Good by Jack Williamson and Mary Ann Salerno (Bridge Builder Media, 2001).

177

Divorce Casualties: Protecting Your Children from Parental Alienation by Douglas Darnall (Taylor, 1998).

Divorce First Aid: How to Protect Yourself from Domestic Violence, Parental Kidnappings, Theft of Property and Other Domestic Emergencies by Webster Watnik (Single Parent Press, 2000).

Divorce Hangover: A Successful Strategy to End the Emotional Aftermath of Divorce by Anne Newton Walther (Tapestries, 2001).

Divorce and New Beginnings: A Complete Guide to Recovery, Solo Parenting, Co-Parenting, and Stepfamilies by Genevieve Clapp (John Wiley & Sons, 2000).

The Divorce Recovery Sourcebook by Dawn Bradley Berry (Contemporary Books, 1999).

The Fresh Start Divorce Recovery Workbook: A Step-by-Step Program for Those Who Are Divorced or Separated by Bob Burns (Thomas Nelson, 1998).

Getting Divorced Without Ruining Your Life: A Reasoned, Practical Guide to the Legal, Emotional, and Financial Ins and Outs of Negotiating a Divorce Settlement by Sam Margulies (Fireside, 2001).

Getting Up, Getting Over, Getting On: A Twelve Step Guide to Divorce Recovery by Micki McWade (Champion Press, 1999).

The Good Divorce: Keeping Your Family Together When Your Marriage Comes Apart by Constance Ahrons (HarperCollins, 1998).

Good Parenting Through Your Divorce: How to Recognize, Encourage, and Respond to Your Child's Feelings and Help Them Get Through Your Divorce by Mary Ellen Hannibal (Marlowe, 2002).

Helping Children Cope with Divorce by Edward Teyber (Jossey-Bass, 2001).

Joint Custody with a Jerk: Raising a Child with an Uncooperative Ex by Julia A. Ross and Judy Corcoran (St. Martin's Press, 1996).

Making Divorce Easier on Your Child by Nicholas Long and Rex Forehand (Contemporary Books, 2002).

Mom's House, Dad's House: Making Two Homes for Your Child by Isolina Ricci (Fireside, 1997).

The Visitation Handbook for the Custodial Parent: Your Complete Guide to Parenting Apart by Brette McWhorter Sember (Sourcebooks, 2002).

What About the Kids? Raising Your Children Before, During, and After Divorce by Judith S. Wallerstein and Sandra Blakeslee (Hyperion Books, 2003).

Your Divorce Advisor: A Lawyer and a Psychologist Guide You Through the Legal and Emotional Landscape of Divorce by Diana Mercer and Marsha Pruett (Fireside, 2001).

Books for Children

At Daddy's on Saturdays by Linda Walvoord Girard (Albert Whitman, 1991).

The Boys and Girls Book About Divorce by Richard Gardner (Bantam Books for Young Readers, 1985).

Dinosaurs Divorce by Laurie Krasny and Marc Brown (Little, Brown & Company, 1988).

Divorce Happens to the Nicest Kids by Michael S. Prokop (Allegra House, 1996).

The Divorce Workbook: An Interactive Guide for Kids and Families by Sally B. Ives, David Fassler, and Michelle Lash (Waterfront Books, 1988).

Help! A Girl's Guide to Divorce and Stepfamilies by Nancy Holyoke (Pleasant Company Publications, 1999).

I Don't Want to Talk About It by Jeanie Franz Ransom (Magination, 2000).

It's Not Your Fault Koko Bear by Vicki Lansky (Book Peddlers, 2003).

Let's Talk About It: Divorce by Fred Rogers (Paper Star, 1998).

Mama and Daddy Bear's Divorce by Cornelia Maude Spelman (Albert Whitman, 1998).

My Mom and Dad Are Getting a Divorce! by Florence Bienenfeld (1stBooks Library, 2002).

Taking Good Care of Yourself: For Teens Going Through Separation and Divorce by Risa J. Garon (Children of Separation and Divorce Center, 1994).

Two Homes by Claire Masurel (Candlewick Press, 2001).

Index

Index